PRINCE WILLIAM

PRINCE WILLIAM

A Biography

Joann F. Price

GREENWOOD BIOGRAPHIES

 GREENWOOD

AN IMPRINT OF ABC-CLIO, LLC
Santa Barbara, California • Denver, Colorado • Oxford, England

Library of Congress Cataloging-in-Publication Data

Price, Joann F.
  Prince William : a biography / Joann F. Price.
    p. cm. — (Greenwood biographies)
  Includes bibliographical references and index.
  ISBN 978-0-313-39285-6 (acid-free paper) — ISBN 978-0-313-39286-3 (ebook) 1. William, Prince, grandson of Elizabeth II, Queen of Great Britain, 1982- 2. Princes—Great Britain—Biography. I. Title.
  DA591.A45W5573 2011
  941.085092—dc22
  [B]   2010053611

ISBN: 978-0-313-39285-6
EISBN: 978-0-313-39286-3

15 14 13 12 11   1 2 3 4 5

This book is also available on the World Wide Web as an eBook.
Visit www.abc-clio.com for details.

Greenwood
An Imprint of ABC-CLIO, LLC

ABC-CLIO, LLC
130 Cremona Drive, P.O. Box 1911
Santa Barbara, California 93116-1911

This book is printed on acid-free paper ∞

Manufactured in the United States of America

For Bob, always and forever. And for our own splendid princes, already more noble than kings.

CONTENTS

SERIES FOREWORD

In response to high school and public library needs, Greenwood developed this distinguished series of full-length biographies specifically for student use. Prepared by field experts and professionals, these engaging biographies are tailored for high school students who need challenging yet accessible biographies. Ideal for secondary school assignments, the length, format, and subject areas are designed to meet educators' requirements and students' interests.

Greenwood offers an extensive selection of biographies spanning all curriculum-related subject areas, including social studies, the sciences, literature and the arts, history, and politics, as well as popular culture, covering public figures and famous personalities from all time periods and backgrounds, both historic and contemporary, who have made an impact on American and/or world culture. Greenwood biographies were chosen based on comprehensive feedback from librarians and educators. Consideration was given to both curriculum relevance and inherent interest. The result is an intriguing mix of the well known and the unexpected, the saints and sinners from long-ago history and contemporary pop culture. Readers will find a wide array of subject choices, from fascinating crime figures such as Al Capone to inspiring pioneers such as Margaret Mead, from the greatest minds of our time such as Stephen Hawking to the most amazing success stories of our day, such as that of J. K. Rowling.

While the emphasis is on fact, not glorification, the books are meant to be fun to read. Each volume provides in-depth information about the subject's life from birth through childhood, the teen years, and adulthood. A thorough account relates family background and education, traces personal and professional influences, and explores struggles, accomplishments, and contributions. A timeline highlights the most significant life events against a historical perspective. Bibliographies supplement the reference value of each volume.

INTRODUCTION

His birth was a highly anticipated event in all of Great Britain in June 1982. About two months later, with the archbishop of Canterbury officiating in the Music Room of Buckingham Palace, the royal baby was christened His Royal Highness Prince William Arthur Philip Louis of Wales. And although other titles were added later, the prince is known familiarly as Will, or Wills, and to his subjects, he is Prince William. As the second in line to the throne, he is destined to be His Royal Highness, King William V. Few could disagree that he is the most popular member of Britain's Royal Family today. With his mother's good looks and his father's intellect, he has been for some time one of the most eligible bachelors in the world, although he became engaged to Kate Middleton in 2010, and because the Royals are known for relatively short engagements, they will marry in spring 2011. Prince William is also known to be serious in nature, quite intelligent, and lighthearted; he is committed to serving others and is respected for his strength of character and for how he has conducted himself in the midst of great tragedy. As the eldest son of Prince Charles of England and the late Princess Diana, this very modern prince is in touch with his contemporaries and is firmly situated as an emerging member of an ever-changing world, while at the same time being someone who strictly guards his privacy. And although he has been groomed to be king from the day of his heralded birth, he has said publicly that he is reluctant to be crowned king yet realizes he has no say in the matter whatsoever.

From the moment of his birth through his academic life, the prince has traveled the world with his father, his late mother, and his younger brother, Prince Harry. He is an ambassador of the Royal Family within his country and around the world, has served in the military, and has lent his name to humanitarian, charitable, and environmental causes. His story, thus far, has been one of near constant scrutiny, public service, and great tragedy. It has also been a life characteristic of a royal, yet at the same time certainly not as typical as those of other members of the British Royal Family throughout its great and long history.

Once described as a "reluctant prince," he has, in many watchers' opinions, surpassed what has been expected of him thus far in his life. His mother, Princess Diana, who is still beloved around the world, once said of her two sons, "William and Harry are my one splendid achievement." Her son the Royal Highness bears an almost uncanny resemblance to his famous and adored mother. And he also is unquestionably loved, recognized, and respected throughout the world. Because he is a role model and a trendsetter, especially among his peer group, what Prince William does and says matters. If he becomes King of England, as many assume he will, this charming man will no doubt be an integral part of a significant and omnipresent reign of influence, an important and influential part of the history of the English Empire, and a leader throughout the world.

Sometime soon, perhaps in the next decade or two, Prince William will be crowned King William V. As from the seventh century on in the hereditary British monarchy, this succession will happen whether William wants it or not, whether he wants to change the line of succession or not. From the moment of his birth, he has been educated and groomed to wear the crown. There are often rumors that Prince Charles will step aside in favor of his eldest son. There are also reports that Queen Elizabeth II, the prince's grandmother, who was crowned in 1952, highly favors her grandson and is slowly transferring some of her duties to him. However, if the history of the monarchy is our guide, and if Prince Charles survives his mother the Queen, Charles will be crowned king, and his elder son, William, will follow.

When William turned 21 years of age in 2003, he was recognized as His Royal Highness and made a Knight of the Thistle. For all of his life, William has known his destiny: he will be king. There is no other role for him. His life has always been carefully supervised, and as an adult, he lives as he is expected to, and every aspect of his life and work is carefully chosen; he must be and remain suitable as the future sovereign of his country. Despite being in a most extraordinary situation, Prince William is known to be a very ordinary man. However, given that his mother, one of the most famous women in the world, was killed in a horrific car crash trying to escape the infamous paparazzi, and his father was involved in one of the most publicized love affairs of the century, and his grandmother is the long-serving and much-admired Queen Elizabeth II, and his great-grandfather was the last Emperor of India, one can hardly describe William as normal. He is a highly visible global traveler, sought after, charismatic, intelligent, intellectual, highly sensitive to the plight of others, and arguably the most popular member of the Royal Family. As someone ardently aware of his position and his future, should he become king sooner rather than later, he will undoubtedly send a quiver throughout the monarchy and around the world.

One of Prince Charles's closest friends said of William, "I think he can make the whole thing work. He's a much tougher character than his father and, because of Diana, he'll have the people with him. He's incredibly nice, you know." A Buckingham Palace courtier agreed: "He seems to know exactly where he is going. He is a bright boy who knows what he wants, assertive but cool at the same time. It is already very clear that he will have a purpose in life that relates to the real world as well as his birthright of the throne."[1]

NOTE

1. Christopher Andersen, *Diana's Boys* (New York: William Morrow, 2001), 318.

TIMELINE: EVENTS IN THE LIFE OF PRINCE WILLIAM

1901	The modern age of the British monarchy begins after the death of Queen Victoria, who died at the age of 101 after reining longer than any monarch in history.
	King Edward VII, Victoria's eldest son, ascends to the throne.
1910	King Edward VII dies. His brother George V ascends to the throne.
1914–1918	World War I.
1926	Elizabeth, the eldest daughter of King George V, is born.
1932	King George V begins regular radio broadcasts to the people of the Commonwealth.
January 1936	King George V dies and his son, Edward VIII, becomes King.
December	King Edward VIII signs the Instrument of Abdication, giving up the throne and renouncing any future claims. His young brother, Albert, ascends to the throne and becomes King George VI. The coronation is held in May 1937.

1939	War breaks out between Great Britain and Germany.
1940	England suffers during the Blitz, when German bombers continually bomb the country and specific areas of London.
December 1941	The United States declares war on Germany and Japan and is an ally of Great Britain.
1945	World War II ends.
November 1947	Elizabeth and Philip are married at Westminster Abbey.
November 14, 1948	Prince Charles is born.
August 15, 1950	Princess Anne is born.
February 1952	King George VI dies of lung cancer. His eldest daughter, Elizabeth, ascends to the throne as Queen Elizabeth II.
February 19, 1960	Prince Andrew is born.
March 10, 1964	Prince Edward is born.
July 29, 1981	Prince Charles and Lady Diana Spencer are married at St. Paul's Cathedral.
January 9, 1982	Catherine (Kate) Middleton is born.
June 21, 1982	William Arthur Philip Louis of Wales, commonly known as Prince William, is born.
September 15, 1984	Henry Charles Albert David of Wales, commonly known as Prince Harry, is born.
September 1990	William enters Ludgrove School, a boarding school in Berkshire.
September 1995	William enters Eton College, near the town of Windsor and Windsor Castle.
August 1996	Prince Charles and Princess Diana officially divorce after a 15-year marriage.
August 31, 1997	Princess Diana dies in Paris.
September 6, 1997	Princess Diana's funeral is held at Westminster Abbey.
June 2000	William finishes his studies at Eton College in June and takes his gap year before entering the University of St. Andrews.

September 2001	William enters the University of St. Andrews in Fife, Scotland, in September. Kate Middleton also enrolls.
March 2002	The Queen Mother dies at the age of 101.
September 2002	William and Kate Middleton begin sharing an apartment while studying at the University of St. Andrews.
April 2005	Prince Charles and Camilla Parker-Bowles marry. Camilla becomes the Duchess of Cornwall.
June 23, 2005	William graduates from the University of St. Andrews. Kate Middleton also graduates.
January 8, 2006	William enters the Royal Military Academy at Sandhurst to begin his training.
December 2006	William graduates from Sandhurst.
January 17, 2008	William completes his first solo flight as he continues his Royal Air Force training.
April 11, 2008	William receives his Royal Air Force wings.
June 2008	William begins a two-month attachment with the Royal Navy.
October 2008	William is appointed Honorary Air Commandant of the Royal Air Force by the Queen.
January 2009	William begins an 18-month training to become a full-time helicopter pilot with the Royal Air Force Search and Rescue Force.
September 2009	William and Harry establish the Foundation for Prince William and Prince Harry as they continue to follow their parents' model of charitable and humanitarian work.
Summer 2010	William successfully completes his training to become a Sea King helicopter pilot with the Royal Air Force.
November 16, 2010	William and Kate hold a press conference to announce their engagement.
November 23, 2010	It is announced that the royal wedding will be held at Westminster Abbey on Friday, April 29, 2011.

Chapter 1

PRINCE WILLIAM'S ANCESTRY

OVERVIEW

From the day he was born, Prince William has been groomed to be King of England. Virtually everything in his upbringing has been planned with the intent that he will someday wear the crown. A biography of this prince, who will someday be known as King William V, also requires study of the history of his ancestors and the realm's past and probable future. This is important because William's very core is deeply influenced by his country's colorful, often violent, and deeply significant monarchy, a kingdom that dates back at least as far as the seventh century.

The future king's realm, known simply as Britain or Great Britain, England, or the United Kingdom, is one of only a few remaining monarchies in the world today. This means that the head of state, the king or queen, inherits the position rather than being elected to it. Today, the monarchy remains at the center of the British realm, and the British Royal Family continues to be omnipresent throughout the country. Whether they are despised or loved, whether they ignore the commoners or travel in the people's midst, the story of the British monarchy is as interesting as it has ever been. Not everyone supports them, of course. There continue to be loud voices calling for an end to the Royal Family's life of privilege in this modern age. However, the people cannot vote them out as they would vote out politicians. The Royals are here to stay, except that they do evolve, they do change with the times, and the next king, whether it is King Charles (known at present as Prince Charles) or his eldest son, William, will rule in a world vastly different from the one in existence when the current Queen Elizabeth II acceded to the throne in 1952. Over the years, England has gradually become more democratic, which has resulted in a shrinking but still prominent ruling Royal Family. This has presented challenges for the monarchy, yet the family still prevails. Today, the Royal Family remains a national symbol, with traditions steeped in history. It respects titles, traditions, old wealth, rights, and privileges.

THE MONARCHY STRUCTURE

Since the 7th century, with only a short break during the 17th century, when the kingdom was a republic, kings and queens have ruled the English empire. The monarch made all the laws and owned most of the land, and disobedience meant treason and likely death. In short, the king or the queen had all the power. Over the course of history, there were many challenges to the sovereign's rule. There were wars, rebellion, and fights for control, both inside the monarchy within the ruling court and throughout the land. Challenges to the monarch's rule also came from outside the realm. Because they were protected by the surrounding seas, throughout history England was invaded only a few times. The powerful British navy was able to keep invaders away, and its commanding sea power enabled Britain to affect world history, to increase the power of the monarchy, and to increase the width and breadth of the English empire.

For centuries, it was said that the sun never set on the British Empire. With British ships sailing around the world, the monarchy gained power in North America, India, Australia, and Africa. From the 17th through the 19th centuries, the British Empire was sovereign over vast lands throughout the world. Over the centuries, to raise money to pay for the royalty, the people were taxed. In order to have their say and to gain at least some power over their lives, the people raised their voices, sometimes to the point of disastrous rebellion; slowly, the monarch's power was usurped, and the people of the realm gained power. This power came in the form of the Parliament, the nation's legislature, and by the 18th century, many of the monarch's powers were taken over by this governing body. Today, the British Empire's reach is much smaller, given that most of the foreign lands the country conquered hundreds of years ago are now independent; still, associations with the monarchy remain. Some of the former colonies have what is called dominion status—Canada, Australia, and New Zealand—where the British sovereign remains the head of state. At one time, South Africa also had dominion status; however, that country now has its own elected president. Other nations have their own heads of state but are part of the Commonwealth—allied nations that effectively replaced the empire. These allied nations began to leave the British Empire after World War II, and in 1958, the Commonwealth was nationally recognized.[1] Queen Elizabeth II, as Queen of England, Scotland, Wales, and Northern Ireland, is the monarch of the Commonwealth and the recognized head of state of 15 of its member nations, including Canada and Australia.

Presently, Britain's Queen Elizabeth is a constitutional monarch, with the real power held by the House of Commons and the House of Lords, collectively known as Parliament. However, unlike the United States, there is no complete written document; the Constitution is a set of rules, some unwritten, some written, as laws are passed by Parliament. Such rules have been established over time, evolving since the 17th century when the Bill of Rights was established. The latter set down key principles to protect the rights of Parliament and limit the power of the ruling monarch, including establishing that taxes could not be levied by royal prerogative alone, that elections of members of Parliament that should take place without royal interference, and that the people of the realm could petition the ruling monarch. Over time, other rules were enacted—for example, that the monarch could not make or pass legislation, must always remain politically neutral, and could not vote in elections; must, in matters of government, always act on the advice of his or her ministers; and cannot enter the branch of Parliament known as the House of Commons.[2]

Although the monarchy remains an important aspect of the very fabric of British life, from the national anthem of "Long Live the Queen" to the government's nomenclature "Her Majesty's Government," Queen Elizabeth II has much less power than her ancestors. Her duties include opening Parliament and giving the traditional monarch's speech, approving acts of Parliament and other governmental measures, reading briefing papers on governmental business, and attending weekly meetings with the prime minister. She also represents Britain to other nations, receives their heads of state, and travels to other countries on state visits. She bestows awards and honors and recognizes achievements of her subjects; supports charitable organizations; leads the nation in times of conflict or sorrow; and through visits throughout the realm, often referred to as "walkabouts," meets with her subjects. The Queen also holds special positions, including the head of the Church of England and roles within the armed services and in England's justice system. Because her list of responsibilities and duties is long, she often delegates official duties to other members of her family, including her son, Prince Charles, and her grandson, Prince William. It is estimated that the Queen and members of her Royal Family attend approximately 2,000 official engagements each year; entertain about 70,000 people at royal parties, dinners, lunches, and receptions during the year; and answer more than 100,000 letters annually. Known also for its charitable work, the Royal Family has a role in about 2,000 charities in Britain.[3]

The Queen and her Royal Family are wealthy and privileged, and because they cannot be voted out of office, they can seemingly do whatever they please; their subjects must obey them, no matter what. However, although this was true in days of old, today the monarchy is well aware of the criticisms of the Royal Family and the factions that believe the monarchy is too costly and should be replaced with a republic, headed by an elected head of state, especially once Queen Elizabeth, now in her eighties, passes away. Detractors are also weary of the class system that still pervades the country and the system of privilege that cannot continue to be justified. Supporters of the monarchy stress that the Queen does not exercise her own political will in political matters and point to the limited role the monarchy plays in government policy, and many even call for a more active role for the

Queen and the next crowned sovereign, Prince Charles, or his eldest son, Prince William. Many agree that the Britons themselves should be given the chance to vote on the monarchy's future.[4]

THE HOUSE OF WINDSOR, THE BEGINNING OF THE MODERN MONARCHY, QUEEN VICTORIA, 1819–1901

Since the early 20th century, the modern monarchy, known as the House of Windsor, has, as throughout history, seen its share of turbulence and transformation. It could be said that the modern age of the monarchy began in 1901, when Queen Victoria, after reigning longer than any other British monarch, died at the age of 81. From her ascension to the throne in 1837, she experienced a difficult beginning to her rule, partly because she was only 18 when she became queen and partly because she was related to the House of Hanover and was associated with its past extravagances and scandals. Victoria was determined to be different from her predecessors and carefully steered clear of the missteps and disgraces that had been a common thread of the monarchies throughout history. During her reign, Victoria presided over a time of great prosperity, a period in which her realm was the center of a worldwide empire and at the forefront of industry and invention. With her husband, Prince Albert, whom she married in 1840, Victoria enacted educational and health reforms that benefited the British people. Queen Victoria and Prince Albert resolutely set an example for their people, and the country improved from all their efforts. Along with arranging marriages throughout Europe for her nine children, Victoria worked steadily for peace during her reign.

In 1861, Prince Albert died, leaving Victoria overwhelmed by grief and incapable of performing her duties. For a time, she insisted that she was too fatigued and not well enough to attend public engagements or to attend matters of state; questions circulated as to whether she was fit to wear the crown, and the idea of changing to a republic flourished. But despite her grief, Victoria was steadfast, and even though she continued to mourn and don only black clothing for the rest of her life, she continued her reign. In 1887, Victoria marked her 50th year on the throne with the Golden Jubilee, a major royal occasion attended by heads of state from all over Europe. Ten years later, she marked the 60th anniversary of her accession with the Diamond Jubilee. This event emphasized the entirety of the British Empire, and representatives from the British colonies, including members of their armed forces, attended the festivities.

There were vast, important changes during Queen Victoria's time on the throne, within her own country and around the world. As an example, when she was born, stage coaches were a prominent mode of transportation. By 1901, a network of railroads existed in England, and in America, the Wright brothers were perfecting their "flying machine." In her later years, the Royal Family found it easier to travel, and the Queen and her family were seen by more people than ever before. With the advent of newspapers and magazines and the invention of photography and motion pictures, there was greater awareness of the Royals and their daily life; her subjects were able to follow her and the family like never before. The world was changing quickly, and for many who found the changes bewildering, the continuation of the monarchy and the Queen herself meant stability and security. By the end of her reign, Queen Victoria ruled over subjects in Canada, Australia and New Zealand, South Africa, and India.

EDWARD VII, 1841–1910

Upon Victoria's death, her eldest son, Albert Edward, at nearly 60 years old, ascended to the throne as Edward VII. As Prince of Wales, he had spent most of his life enjoying a pleasurable existence, including playing bridge, going to the theater, hunting, and horse racing. With a lifestyle that had included numerous relationships, lots of parties, extensive foreign travel, and a rebellion against his parents' strict morals and values, along with what many thought were undisciplined work habits, he was seemingly not prepared for the job of sovereign of the English empire. However, his social skills made him a popular ruler. In 1863, he married Princess Alexandra, the eldest daughter of the king of Denmark, and his subjects responded to him and the Royal Family positively; always wanting to be the center of society, Edward found himself out in public often, and his subjects adored him and his Royal Family of five children. Edward died in 1910 and was widely mourned.

His public turned out throughout London to pay their respects to a king who made the monarchy more symbolic and less political as the country entered the 20th century.[5]

GEORGE V, 1865–1936

The next in line to the throne was George V, a man who had never expected to be king. Because he was the second son of Edward and Alexandra, his older brother, Albert Victor, was the expected successor; however, Albert Victor died in 1892, and George found himself in line to the throne. George had spent 15 years in the navy, and upon his brother's death, he reluctantly took on the duties of politics. Being shy and disliking parties and receptions, he was seemingly ill-suited to be the sovereign. He tended to follow his grandparents' more conservative views and rejected his own father's more libertine lifestyle and attitudes; however, he did have a loving relationship with both parents. Having never married, when he became the future king after his brother's death, he was expected to marry his late brother's fiancée, Princess May (Mary), which he did in 1893. Despite being a somewhat arranged marriage, it became one of great affection.

Four years into his reign, George had the unenviable task of leading his nation through the turbulent and deadly Great War, World War I, which lasted from 1914 to 1918. Britain and Germany were the two main powers involved in this bloody conflict, and the Royal Family had always had close personal ties to Germany. As a result, the monarchy was deeply involved in the great miseries caused by the long and costly war. The widespread hatred of Germans created problems for the King and the Royal Family. To lessen the anti-monarchy feelings, the King openly and often made his support of the English troops known, making numerous visits to the battlefields. Acknowledging the anti-German feelings in Britain, and realizing prejudices and reminders of the royal Germanic roots created by the Royal Family's name of Saxe-Coburg, a name inherited from the King's father, King George chose to change his family name to Windsor. The King's secretary suggested the new name, which had links to the ancient castle where the Royal Family had lived since the Middle Ages. The new name was quintessentially "British." The name change proved to be a success because it was a signal to the people of the realm that the Royal Family was solidly British.[6] Further, the King imposed a ban on alcohol in all palaces during the war to set an example for the nation, and along with everyone else in England, the royal household maintained its share of rationed items. The King also stated that in the future, members of the Royal Family would be allowed to marry into British families. Some felt this allowance was an extreme measure, but most welcomed the closer identification of the monarchy with the nation.[7] When the war ended, King George took a leading role in commemorating those who had been killed in the war with the tradition of remembering them on November 11, the day the armistice was signed.[8]

The reign of George V was one of change, of turbulence, and sacrifice, and it also saw the beginning of the end of the vast British Empire. In 1931, Parliament formulated the Statute of Westminster, which created the idea of a Commonwealth of Nations. This created the pathway for many nations of the empire to become independent of the realm while maintaining a relationship with Britain through the Commonwealth. Another change instituted by the King was that of making regular radio broadcasts, which took the Royal Family into people's homes in a new way. The broadcasts began at Christmas in 1932. These broadcasts were deemed very successful, with the message enhancing understanding and communication between the diverse nations of the British Empire. Since that first holiday message in 1932, every monarch has broadcast a special message to the nation at Christmas, on the radio and on television.[9]

EDWARD VIII, 1894–1972

Over the course of the history of the monarchy, most if not all kings and queens were obsessed over their successor and what qualities the next monarch would bring to the throne. This was also the case for George V, who, during his last years, worried that his eldest son, David, later known as Edward, the Prince of Wales, would not be a "good" king. King George remarked to Stanley Baldwin, the prime minister at the time, "After I am dead, the boy will ruin himself in twelve months."[10]

Though named Edward Albert Christian George Andrew Patrick David, as a young man, the future king was known to his friends and at home simply as David until his father became king, at which time he was made the Prince of Wales and became known as Edward. In his youth, Edward spent time at the Naval College and studied at Oxford, and during World War I, he served on the western front but was not allowed to fight because he was heir to the throne. In the years following the war, he traveled throughout the Commonwealth and also visited New York, where he was given a rousing reception. All of his travels were watched closely by his father; after all, he was being groomed to be king, and much was expected of him. For the most part, his father felt his appearances were worthy and even positive, except for his visits to New Zealand and India, where his father criticized him for being not properly attired and for altering his dress without prior approval.

As the eldest of six children, Edward felt the brunt of his father's dominance, and his relationship with his father was often particularly tense. Edward found his father's devotions to detail and ceremony tedious and out of touch in a postwar world, which he felt was now more relaxed. As well, the lifestyles of King George and his eldest son were vastly different. The King's life centered on family, routine, and devotion to the monarchy. Prince Edward, on the other hand, was unmarried, showed no sign of wanting to marry, and was restless. He enjoyed playing golf and hunting, and his taste for dining and dancing was well known; he was regularly seen enjoying an active social life that included attending London nightclubs. Whereas the King's personality closely followed that of the King's grandmother, Queen Victoria, Edward's personality and lifestyle was likened to that of Edward's grandfather, Edward VII. Like him, Edward was fair-haired and had a slight build, but unlike Edward VII, he could also be inpatient, self-occupied, and obstinate and was often thought to be bored in his duties once he acceded to the throne. It was often thought that Edward never wanted to be king; however, because he greatly enjoyed the privileged life the position gave him, it is more likely he did want to be king, but a king on his own terms, which included being a less ceremonial and less traditional monarch.

Throughout the history of the monarchy, the king or queen has always been expected to marry a suitable partner and produce an heir; this was one of their most basic, inherent duties. Prince Edward showed no signs of marrying or producing the next in line to the throne. In fact, he was often seen in the company of married women. In 1930, through a friend, Edward was introduced to Wallis Simpson, an American woman married to a British shipping broker. By 1934, Mrs. Simpson had Edward's constant attention, and the two were clearly in love. In 1935, Edward wrote to Mrs. Simpson, "I love you more & more & more each & every minute & miss you so terribly here. You do too don't you my sweetheart?"[11] Many monarchy watchers were worried because Edward was in love with the most "unsuitable" of partners, an American divorcee. In January 1936, when King George V died, the Prince of Wales became King Edward VIII, and he wanted Mrs. Simpson to be his queen. However, the archbishop of Canterbury, the prime minister, many in Parliament, and Edward's own mother thought a marriage to Mrs. Simpson, a divorced American, was out of the question, especially because as king, he was the head of the Church of England, and in that context alone, marrying a divorcee was not acceptable. Despite all of this, Edward carried on and was sure that the public would accept his actions, and in the summer of 1936, the controversy came to a close.

In America, the couple's friendship and later love affair were covered with interest and speculation; however, in England, a gentlemen's agreement with the media kept much of their relationship out of the newspapers for the greater part of 1936.[12] In August 1936, Edward and Wallis embarked on a cruise. Their trip was covered extensively by writers and photographers and eagerly followed by readers of both American and British newspapers. After the trip, Mrs. Simpson filed for divorce, and she stayed with the King at Balmoral, the King's royal Scottish home. In October, the divorce came through, and as a result, she was free to marry the King. Throughout this time, the government, including the cabinet and the prime minister, Stanley Baldwin, discussed the constitutionality of the proposed marriage and of Mrs. Simpson becoming queen. The cabinet had a right to warn against the marriage, and should the warning not be heeded, they could tender their resignations, and a new government would have to be formed. Additionally, there was doubt as to whether the Church of England, which did not officially accept divorce, could take any ceremonial part in such a marriage. By the middle of October, the prime minister was trying to head off an impending crisis over the matter. He gave the King a file of press clippings that clearly left no doubt about the gossip. During this time, Baldwin, as prime minister, held meetings with leaders of the political parties, who were all in agreement that Mrs. Simpson was not suitable to be queen. On November 16, the prime minister told the King that his proposed marriage to Mrs. Simpson would not be acceptable to the government. The King responded that he would abdicate if he was not allowed to marry.[13] On December 10, 1936, King Edward VIII signed the Instrument of Abdication, a document where he gave up the throne and renounced any claim to the throne on the part of any of his future heirs. The day after, Edward spoke to the nation, explaining he would not be king because Wallis would not be beside him as queen. The country was stunned, especially because the public had been shielded from many of the details of the King's relationships with Mrs. Simpson. Edward left the country for France, where he married Wallis Simpson the next year. This was the beginning of decades away from his family and his country. King Edward VIII became the Duke of Windsor, and Wallis became the Duchess of Windsor.

KING GEORGE VI, 1895–1952

Many in government and close to the monarchy feared that Edward's abdication would deal a blow to the monarchy; however, the monarchy continued, partly because in his radio broadcast to the country, Edward had asked for the people's support of his brother and stated that his brother was ready to succeed. He said of him, "And he has one matchless blessing, enjoyed by so many of you and not bestowed on me—a happy home with his wife and children."[14] Prince Albert ascended to the throne the day after Edward abdicated and chose to reign as George VI. Although he was a shy man and was generally in awe of his newfound responsibilities and obligations, and even though he had a strong dislike of appearing in public and had never wanted to be king, he was devoted to his duties. Christened Albert Frederick Arthur George, at home and as a boy he was known as Albert, or familiarly as Bertie. Like his older brother, he was brought up mainly by a nanny and had a rather distant relationship with his parents, King George V and Queen Mary. Afflicted with health problems from an early age, young Albert also was fitted with splints to wear every night to correct "knock-knees," and additionally, even though he was left-handed, he was forced to write with his right hand. All of these problems together contributed to the shyness of a young man afflicted with a stammer that lasted until adulthood.

Like many before him, Albert served in the Royal Navy. Despite an illness that threatened his career, he did serve on board ship during World War I, and after the war he continued to serve in the armed forces, this time in the Royal Air Force. Knowing that his older brother was in line to be king, and never expecting to be considered as handsome or as charismatic as his brother was, he decided to use his strong sense of duty and travel the country getting to know the people and their lives. He worked on various social programs to assist people in difficult economic times, including becoming a patron of the Industrial Welfare Society and setting up the Duke of York's camps, meeting places for boys from the working classes. The camps proved to be very popular and continued until 1939 and the beginning of World War II. His work was considered helpful in making the Royal Family less remote and more interested in the lives of ordinary people.[15]

In 1923, Albert married Lady Elizabeth Bowes-Lyon, the daughter of Scottish aristocrats. Whereas he was shy and often withdrawn, she was outgoing and vivacious, making her an ideal mate to help him overcome his dislike for making speeches. They did share common interests, despite their difference in personalities, including a love of the outdoors. Theirs was not an arranged marriage, as nearly all marriages were in the history of the monarchy; it was one of devotion and partnership. To the public and also in private, they were genuinely a loving couple. Their marriage soon produced two daughters, Elizabeth, the future queen, born in 1926, and Margaret Rose, born in 1930. In a short while, this Royal Family was thought to be one of strong family values, giving the monarchy a more positive image.

King George VI had never thought he would become king and initially felt unprepared for the role. Although he was well traveled and in touch with the people of his country, he was not as politically or constitutionally astute as he felt he needed to be. The abdication had been costly to the monarchy's image; even though the crown had survived, the gossip surrounding his older brother's affair and subsequent marriage had been very unpleasant for the Royal Family. King George was determined to work to overcome the effects and to restore confidence in the monarchy. As his coronation took place in May 1937, the country was embroiled in the possibility of yet another war with Germany. The new prime minister, Neville Chamberlain, had a policy of avoiding war by appeasing Germany, and George was known to generally feel the same, along with most of the country at the time. In hopes of rallying allied support, George and Elizabeth traveled to France and to the United States. War broke out between Britain and Germany in 1939; the next year, Germany invaded France, Chamberlain resigned, and Winston Churchill became prime minister. In 1940, England suffered greatly during the Blitz, when German bombers continually bombed the country, including specific areas of London. Having served during World War I, George once again donned his uniform, even though he was not able to serve. Instead, he visited troops and the burned-out sections of London and attempted to raise morale. His oldest daughter, Elizabeth, served in the armed forces by joining the Auxiliary Territorial Service (ATS) when she turned 18. Although they could have, as the Royal Family, retreated to the country to various estates for relative safety, they did not. The family stayed in London, and when Buckingham Palace was struck by a bomb, the family narrowly escaped. Having visited many bombed-out sites throughout the city, and staying in London during the worst of the bombing, the King and Queen gradually won the great respect of their people. The war ended in 1945, leaving Britain to recover from years of bombing and from seven years of everything going to the war effort, leaving little if anything in regard to industry and home life. The King and Queen carried on with rebuilding Britain and leading the country to prosperity. The war years left the King in poor health, and in 1951, he was diagnosed with lung cancer. After surviving an operation, he was generally weakened, and in February 1952, at the age of 56, he died in his sleep. His eldest daughter, Elizabeth, who had taken on many of the responsibilities in her father's stead, became queen. George's reign had been dominated by war, and yet through his great efforts of presenting a positive image and personal steadfastness, and together with a family that from the beginning was very close, the reign was considered successful, and he died well loved by his people.

QUEEN ELIZABETH II, 1926–PRESENT: A MODERN MONARCHY

When Elizabeth was 21 years of age, she was granted permission by her father to marry Philip, the nephew of Lord Mountbatten. They had met in Greece in 1939, when Elizabeth was only 13. Philip, at 18, was her third cousin and had just started his naval training. The two maintained a correspondence throughout World War II and by 1944 were in love. After their wedding ceremony at Westminster Abbey in November 1947, the King wrote to his daughter: "Our family, us four, the 'Royal Family' must remain together, with additions of course at suitable moments! . . . your leaving us has left a great blank in our lives but do remember that your old home is still yours."[16] A year later, Prince Charles was born, and in 1950, Princess Anne was born. Elizabeth and Philip had two more children, Andrew, born in 1960, and Edward, in 1964.

In the later part of the 1940s through 1952, as King George's health was failing, Elizabeth began taking on more of his responsibilities, despite having two children. Elizabeth was only 25 years old when, in 1952, her father died and she ascended to the throne and became Queen Elizabeth II. Today, as a constitutional monarch, and at a time when Parliament rules the country, Elizabeth, unlike her ancestor Queen Victoria, who ruled over a world empire, is more of a symbolic figurehead and has only modest power to make policy or change the way her country is governed. She still opens Parliament each year, makes a speech in which she presents the policies of her government, and has weekly meetings with the prime minister, yet her power is vastly different from the powers held by her ancestors.

When she was born in 1926, there was little notion that she would someday be queen. Her uncle, the Prince of Wales, was the eldest son of the current queen and thereby the heir, and he would likely have a son who would inherit the throne. No one could have guessed what would happen over the next decade—that her uncle would abdicate and her father would become king. Suddenly, the young Elizabeth became more popular and certainly gained worldwide attention.

Queen Elizabeth can trace her ancestry beyond Edgar, king of the English in the late 10th century. Her coronation at Westminster Abbey in 1953 was, in many ways, very much like Edgar's coronation held at Bath, England, in 973. But this royal ancestor ruled over a kingdom of approximately 1 million subjects; today, Elizabeth is queen to more than 100 million people and is head of the Commonwealth, with a population of more than a billion. During Edgar's reign, he could be heard by a few hundred subjects at one time and was recognizable to only a few hundred more.[17] To be sure, a land of carts, buckets, shields, and spears has given way to instant gratification, instantaneous communication, a 24-hour news cycle, and continual advances in medicine, warfare, and technology; however, as quick and as oftentimes bewildering as the world's changes are, the threads of the monarchy's continuity remain.

Elizabeth ascended to the throne as her country was rebuilding after the war. Since then, she has governed during a time of significant changes in the Commonwealth and around the world. As well, her family arguably has been more scrutinized and exposed and has probably weathered more difficulties than other royal families in history; at least these difficulties are more well-known than those of years past. The monarchy, for the first time in its history, has had to change with the times, including in its relationship with the media. Regularly, the lives of the Royal Family have been in the glare of the media's eye, oftentimes to the family's detriment and sometimes resulting in great sorrow. Still, Queen Elizabeth, now in her eighties, continues as she always has, with a steel reserve and a dedication to duty and country. Her work continues with receptions, audiences, investitures, opening ceremonies, state visits, and the reading of official documents that continually demand her attention. Every eye and all attentions are always on Elizabeth as queen; careful preparations and extreme attention to ceremony and to history are always topmost in the Queen's daily life and governance. As with most heads of state, and like her ancestors, the Queen values her personal time with family and when she can be away from the center of government and in the country with her dogs and horses. Hers has been a modern monarchy, one of global change and one not without tragedy, scandal, and certainly successes. Although she has reigned under intense and constant view, and although scandals have plagued her and her family, the monarchy continues. The scandals and tragedies over the past century have afforded ammunition to those who wish to abolish the monarchy, especially once the Queen leaves the throne, yet she herself has remained distant from her own personal scandals and has not purposely addressed much of what has happened within her court and family, and since her ascension in 1952, few if any have truly questioned Elizabeth's dedication to her work, her country, and her people.

NOTES

1. Philip Wilkinson, *The British Monarchy for Dummies* (Chichester, West Sussex, England: Wiley, 2006), 12–15.

2. Ibid., 24.

3. Ibid., 29–30.

4. Kenneth Jost, "The British Monarchy," *CQ Researcher Online* 6, no. 9 (March 8, 1996), 195–96, http://library.cqpress.com/cqresearcher/cqresrre1996030800 (accessed February 25, 2010).

5. Philip Wilkinson, *The British Monarchy for Dummies* (Chichester, West Sussex, England: Wiley, 2006), 275.

6. Ibid., 281.

7. John Cannon and Ralph Griffiths, *The Oxford Illustrated History of the British Monarchy* (Oxford, England: Oxford University Press, 1988), 591–92.

8. Philip Wilkinson, *The British Monarchy for Dummies* (Chichester, West Sussex, England: Wiley, 2006), 282.

9. Ibid., 284–85.

10. John Cannon and Ralph Griffiths, *The Oxford Illustrated History of the British Monarchy* (Oxford, England: Oxford University Press, 1988), 600.

11. Ibid., 604.

12. Ibid., 603.

13. Ibid., 603, 605.

14. Ibid., 606.

15. Philip Wilkinson, *The British Monarchy for Dummies* (Chichester, West Sussex, England: Wiley, 2006), 291–92.

16. John Cannon and Ralph Griffiths, *The Oxford Illustrated History of the British Monarchy* (Oxford, England: Oxford University Press, 1988), 614.

17. Ibid., 631–32.

Chapter 2

A HERALDED PRINCE IS BORN

Princess Diana once said that there was one thing she and Charles had agreed on—that William would have as normal an upbringing as possible. Of course, one wonders what this can mean. How can a baby, or a toddler, boy, or teenager, or even an adult, whose whole life has been carefully orchestrated to prepare him to be a future king, have any sort of a normal upbringing?

Prince William was born on the evening of June 21, 1982. Weighing in at just over seven pounds, William Arthur Philip Louis of Wales instantly made history, not just because he was already second to the British throne and would someday be the sovereign king, but simply because he was the first royal heir born in a hospital and not in a royal residence. It was Princess Diana and her doctor who persuaded Prince Charles that their child should be born in a private wing of a London hospital because there all the modern medical equipment would be available. In the end, this decision was prudent. Diana endured about 16 hours of labor, and it was likely that she would have been transferred to a hospital as a result. The decision for a hospital birth was popular with the media and the public. For the media, access to the princess and the heir was immediate because neither mother nor baby was sequestered behind castle or palace walls. For the public, it was a sure sign that this baby would instantly be introduced to and then raised in a world vastly different from that of his family and ancestors.

The news of William's birth passed quickly throughout the Royal Family, with Queen Elizabeth, baby William's grandmother, receiving the news first. After the news had been passed along among the Royals and to Diana's family, whose father stated that he was "over the moon" about having a new grandson, an official announcement was posted on the gates of Buckingham Palace, where crowds always gather. Even larger crowds had convened for this joyful and momentous event, however—that is, for the news of the birth of a future king. The prime minister was notified as well, along with the members of Parliament; the heads of state of the Commonwealth nations were also informed. Prince Charles, the thrilled father, stated, "The birth of our son has given us both more pleasure than you can imagine. It has made me incredibly proud and somewhat amazed."[1] The first pictures of the new prince were taken not long after his birth when Diana and Charles took the baby home to Kensington Palace, where the young prince would live for the next 16 years.

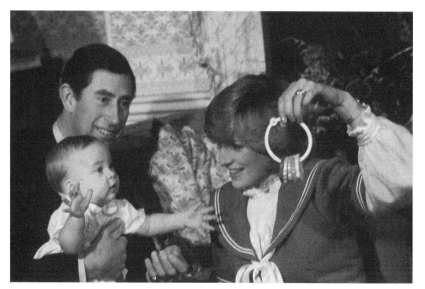

Princess Diana and Prince Charles are shown with their son Prince William during a photo session at Kensington Palace in London in December 1982. (AP Photo/file)

Throughout the history of the monarchy, the name given to a member of the Royal Family has been something seriously considered and steeped in tradition. This was certainly the case for William. Diana favored a modern name, one that was fashionable for the time. Charles and the Queen insisted on a traditional royal name, one that was appropriate for a future king and that had been used throughout history. It seemed that the name William was perfect, a royal name going back to William the Conqueror. Diana, certain that her young son should have a modern name, shortened the name to Wills. She later added yet another name, the playful nickname of Wombat. With the Archbishop of Canterbury officiating, William was christened on August 4, 1982, in the music room of Buckingham Palace. The chosen godparents included King Constantine of the Hellenes and Princess Alexandra; Lady Susan Hussey, a long-serving lady-in-waiting to the Queen; and Natalia, also known as Tally, the Duchess of Westminster, a longtime friend of Charles and Diana.

As the second in line to the throne, William is very much an English prince. His lineage determines that he is the most English member of the royal family since Elizabeth I, with 39 percent of his blood being pure English, with the remainder being Irish, Scottish, American, and German.[2] If William succeeds Prince Charles as king, he will be the 63rd monarch of England and the 44th since the Norman Conquest of 1066.[3]

Although there were nannies at Kensington Palace to care for the young prince, Diana and Charles were determined to be hands-on parents. The nannies cared for him on a day-to-day basis, but Diana and Charles enjoyed bath and feeding times and tried to be present during the daily routines whenever possible. As the Prince and Princess, both Charles and Diana had seemingly never-ending duties, which often took them away from the palace and their son. It was just a few weeks after his birth that an extended trip to Australia was scheduled, and the Queen felt young William should stay at home to be cared for by his nannies. Diana was determined not to leave William at home; if she was to go on the trip, so was the baby. And so it was that William took his first trip abroad. As the pictures of William being carried by his nanny down the steps of the airplane in Australia were broadcast, the public reacted favorably to Diana taking the baby on the trip.

Nannies, of course, have always played an important role in the rearing of children of the Royal Family. It was the same for William. His nannies certainly played a vital role in his life. Although Charles and Diana enjoyed being with William during the day, it was the nanny who took him for walks throughout the gardens at Kensington Palace and who attended him in his nursery. With a security guard always discreetly present, the nanny and William, comfortable in his pram, strolled in the gardens, meeting other nannies or mothers with their children in tow. Sometimes it was the nanny who paid dearly when young William misbehaved. During a trip to Balmoral, the Queen's summer residence, when he was not yet two years old, William pressed a button that alerted the police to the castle. His nanny was blamed for allowing the child to disrupt the expected tranquility at the residence; for their part, Charles and Diana thought the incident was merely something a child does. For sure, his parents, and more specifically Diana, and the nannies typically doted on young William, and the result was often that he could do whatever he pleased. Although Prince Charles certainly loved his son and doted on him in his own way, he was more inclined to enforce a stricter discipline, a manner of child nurturing that harkened back to his own young life. When Charles was a boy, children were more seen and not heard, and although he did not adhere strictly to this form of upbringing, he did expect his son to be raised in a less relaxed manner than was often evidenced in the palace.

When his brother, Prince Harry, was born, William was of an age where he knew his own life had changed. With a little brother taking away some of the attention, combined with his own high-spirited nature, William began to treat his nannies and the servant staff with less respect and good manners than were expected of him. Diana determined that her son's actions were merely those of a mischievous little boy, and his behavior was a part of growing up. Charles determined that more disciplined was needed, believing that everyone should be treated with respect and politeness, as he had been taught as a youngster. Around the time he was three years old, William found himself for the first time being disciplined when he was naughty, by the household staff, by his nannies, and even by his parents, although he remained the center of attention and the center of his mother's life.

A FIRST BIRTHDAY

For many children, the first birthday is a big event, celebrated with family and friends. In comparison with all the exclamations and celebrations that had welcomed him into the world, William's first birthday in June 1983 nearly came and went without any fanfare. To be sure, it was more ordinary than might be expected. Diana and Charles were on a two-week visit to Canada, so the commemoration of the event was left to the nanny, Barbara Barnes, and her assistant, who quietly celebrated the first birthday as an ordinary day for a one-year-old. The separation from his parents did cause some royal watchers consternation, especially the Canadians, who had hoped to get a glimpse of the boy prince. Prince Charles's press officer stated at the time, "There will be a lot of disappointment [on the part of Canadians hoping for a glimpse of William], but the Prince and Princess are unhappy too. They felt the trip is too short to take Prince William. They will be spending much of their time on the royal yacht Britannia and the seas can get pretty rough this time of year."[4] Royal family watchers on London's famous Fleet Street had already taken up speculation about "William at One" and about "the year's most exclusive party," a party everyone thought would be a gala event at the palace. Because of their absence on June 21, Charles and Diana decided a party would be held on July 10, when most of the Royal Family would be together, including cousins and, of course, the nannies.

When William, or Wills as he was known, turned one, he was described as an affectionate, high-spirited child who was being raised as normally as possible and in a manner that was much less formal than the raising of the royal children before him. Diana's father, Earl Spencer, said of his grandson, "The very fact that he sees so much of his mother and father—and that they refuse to be separated from him unless it is really necessary—is different from what even Prince Charles experienced." He further described the parents as "quite potty" over Wills, and it was noted that Diana phoned nanny Barbara Barnes twice a day whenever she was away from her son.[5]

THE PRINCE HAS A BROTHER

On September 15, 1984, William's brother, Prince Henry Charles Albert David of Wales, to be known as Prince Harry, was born. The morning after, William was taken to the hospital to meet his brother for the first time. After waving from the hospital steps to the gathered photographers and reporters, he was taken to his mother's private room, where he met his new brother. For two-year-old William, the birth of a brother meant someone else getting some the attention that he was used to, and Harry's arrival, for a time at least, seemed to intensify William's misbehaviors. Despite the possibility of sibling rivalry at some point developing, William's first meeting with his new brother was the first step to a deep brotherly bond that continues to this day.

OFF TO NURSERY SCHOOL

As a toddler, William was known to be full of spirit and more than a little mischievous. In November 1983, Charles said of his first son, "William is a splendid little character and very good-natured. He seems

Holding hands with Royal nanny Barbara Barnes, Prince William, elder son of Prince Charles and Princess Diana, unseen, leaves St. Mary's Hospital in London on September 16, 1984, after visiting his newborn baby brother, Prince Henry, later known as Prince Harry. (AP Photo/Joseph Schaber)

to have quite a good sense of humour and he is very outgoing."[6] Charles thought he should be disciplined more, and Diana, though at first reluctant, eventually agreed that there should be more discipline and that William needed to learn how to behave with children his own age. She also decided that now that he was a toddler, the first stage of his education should begin. The idea of nursery school appealed to Diana; however, Charles had to be convinced. He did not see the merit of his son attending school away from the palace, instead of following the path of his own at-home education with a governess providing private lessons. In the end, Charles was persuaded to allow William to attend nursery school, after the Queen had been consulted on the matter. Before the school and program were selected, visits were made to several schools, the security service was consulted, and friends and family members were asked for recommendations. Once a school was selected, Mrs. Mynor's Nursery School, located in the area of London known as Nottinghill Gate, security checks were administered. The school was near the palace, and the route to get there was through the palace gardens. Before her son's first day at the school, Diana personally wrote and spoke to each of the parents, apologizing in advance if William's presence disrupted their children's daily routine. Charles asked all the national newspaper editors to provide young William appropriate space and privacy. Despite this request, on his first day of school on September 24, 1985, nearly 150 reporters and photographers were outside the school's doors. To be sure, with a royal in their midst, the school's daily routines were now different. A full-time guard was present, security systems were updated, and a panic button and bullet-proof glass were installed. For his part, young Wills, at just three years of age, was not at all bothered by all the preparations or by the gathered crowd anticipating his arrival.[7] He was, however, insistent on selecting what he would wear for his first day at school. Adorned in a red-checked shirt, red shorts, and red shoes, "he was," Diana noted, "just so excited by it all. He was so organised that he chose his own shorts and shirt. It's best to let him do that if you want him to smile at the cameras."[8] While at Mrs. Mynor's, William acted in two nursery school plays, attended by his parents and younger brother Prince Harry, and also sang a musical solo.

THE BEGINNING OF THE YOUNG PRINCE'S ROYAL DUTIES

As William grew older, the innocent pleasures of nursery school were left behind. Gradually, he was introduced to his formal responsibilities and the roles that were, by the very nature of his sovereignty, predetermined. His mother, however, was resolute in allowing him to transition from childhood to adulthood, from being a boy to being a royal, as gently and as naturally as possible, even though all attempts to encourage him to fit in with ordinary people contained the very clear message that royalty was in his blood. When he turned four in June 1986, William still was not trusted to behave as impeccably as was expected of him. Up until then, young William had had little to do besides being a precocious toddler. He had performed well as he waved from balconies or smiled as he held his mother's hand while walking out of airplanes. Still, because he was known as having rather erratic behavior and to be somewhat of a bully to his young friends at nursery school, it was felt that he was not yet ready to perform official duties at turning four years old, unlike his ancestors, who had been reared to be ready for formal appearances by the time they were three years old.

At home, however, there were seemingly no behavior problems. In 1986, at his birthday party, he and his schoolmates and relatives were entertained by a puppeteer. One party attendee noted, "It was a riot, and William was really squealing with pleasure."[9] Away from home, how he would behave was often another matter. When Diana decided to take him to one of Charles's polo matches near Windsor Castle two weeks after his birthday party, without a nanny to accompany her, William's behavior was difficult at best. He was full of questions and demands: "Where are the horses?" "Can I have ice cream?" "Where are the polo balls?" "I want a drink!" Diana tried in vain to keep hold of him and also chat with family and friends, while he made faces, refused to sit still, and at times leaned out of the balcony so far that Diana had to repeatedly pull him in by the seat of his pants. Clearly frustrated at her son's behavior, Diana carried him to her car and returned to Windsor Castle, where, united with his younger brother Harry, he was much less trouble and far easier to manage. Diana noted, "William's very enthusiastic about things. He pushed himself right into it. Harry is quieter and just watches. No. 2 skates in quite nicely. But the bad luck about being No. 1 is trial and error, so we're open-minded about William."[10]

Despite William's high spirits, and in spite of his parents' relative open-mindedness about his behavior, both Charles and Diana attempted continually to instruct the little prince in royal etiquette and tried to keep him as level-headed as was possible. As a young prince, his life was a series of spectacular events along with rather quiet times at his royal home. There were approximately 40 servants at the palace, and his upbringing, and that of his younger brother, easily could have been turned over to them; however, Diana spent as much time as possible with them, teaching them to swim, picking William up at school, and having lunch together. Charles also spent a great deal of time with both boys and often visited William's school; his relationship with his sons was unusually close, and his method of childrearing was vastly different from that of his own parents, Queen Elizabeth and Prince Philip.

Just after his fourth birthday, William took on his first official duty as part of the Royal Family when he followed the bridesmaids down the aisle at the wedding of his uncle, Prince Andrew, the second son of the Queen, and his bride, Sarah Ferguson. Even though the couple had known each other since childhood, their romance had blossomed after Princess Diana brought them together at a party at Windsor Castle. After a short engagement, the wedding took place on July 23, 1986. As charming and outgoing as the little prince always was, it was anyone's guess how he would perform his duties as a royal pageboy, and extra coaching for the precocious youngster was clearly in order. Dressed in a white sailor's suit and wearing a straw boater hat, William behaved in a way that was expected but less than what was hoped for. While the other boys and girls, all dressed in the finest clothes fit for a royal wedding and, behaved well, William fidgeted and took to sticking out his tongue at the little girls and at the bridesmaids. He also fancied the elastic band on his straw hat, snapping it at anyone nearby. Although his spirited behavior could have been the result of his feeling the ongoing tensions between his parents, it also could have been that he was clearly getting the attention he wanted, and he was also becoming accustomed to his royal social status. After all, he was barely four years old, and a royal wedding at Westminster was something of a milestone for young William.

When William was five years old, he was presented with a few changes. He was enrolled in a new school, and he had a new nanny. By this time, his behavior was thought to be getting out of hand, and his mother blamed everyone but herself. In her eyes, it was the nanny, Barbara Barnes, who was to blame. As his nanny, she too had spoiled William, and because she was a servant, she could not defend herself or answer Diana when blamed. When Diana made the decision to let Ms. Barnes go, she said it was because the nanny was not able to control William. She had become a very important person in William's life, and this did not sit particularly well with Diana. So, by William's fifth birthday, Barbara Barnes was let go, and a new nanny was hired. At first, William was heartbroken and could not be consoled. However, it did not take long for William and his brother Harry to quickly take to Nanny Ruth Wallace, who had been recommended by the family of one of Prince Charles's closest friends, King Constantine. She was known as someone who could easily disregard nonsense from anyone, including spoiled children, and who would use a firm hand while at the same time offering encouragement and stressing self-reliance to her charges. She also believed in the politeness of royal princes, something that gave Prince Charles great relief. Within weeks of her arrival at the palace, she fulfilled all the hopes and expectations for an appropriate nanny for William and Harry.[11]

In January 1987, when William was just four, he left Mrs. Mynor's Nursery School for the Wetherby School, also located in west London and also close to Kensington Palace. By the age of five, William was popular with his classmates and was taking part in school activities and sports. After learning how to swim at Buckingham Palace when he could barely walk, swimming became one of his strongest sports. At the age of seven, he was awarded the Grunfield Cup, a trophy awarded to the boy with the best overall swimming style. Also while at Wetherby, he began to display his competitive spirit. He enjoyed winning, and merely participating was not at all enough for him. As a young prince and the heir to the throne, he continued to be in the spotlight, and he used this while participating in sports and in various other school activities. The young prince demonstrated an aptitude in English and spelling and also displayed a talent for singing. At Wetherby, he sang in Christmas concerts, performing favorite songs such as "The Little Drummer Boy," and was a percussionist with his classmates in performing "Silent Night" and "In the Bleak Midwinter."

ANOTHER NEW NANNY ENTERS THE HOUSEHOLD

In December 1992, it was announced that Charles and Diana had officially separated. A few months later, when William was 10, Alexandra Legge-Bourke, known as Tiggy, was hired by Prince Charles as an assistant private secretary. In a short while, she found herself doing no administrative or secretarial work, but instead was a companion to William and Harry. Tiggy's family had a long history of serving in the royal household, including her mother and aunt, who had both served as ladies-in-waiting. Tiggy had been brought up in South Wales, where she hunted, fished, and enjoyed all manner of rural country recreation. Just like her new charges, she had begun riding horses about as soon as she could walk. In Tiggy, both boys found an older sister they had never had. Within a few weeks, William, who had been nervous around strangers, felt totally relaxed with Tiggy. The boys shared jokes with her and delighted in her seemingly never-ending raucous laughter. When the boys went skiing with Charles, Tiggy went too. And when Tiggy visited her home in Wales, William and Harry went along. At her family home, they could enjoy privacy and freedom. Soon, William depended on Tiggy for nearly everything. He could tell her anything, and she would not laugh or disapprove. It seemed that with her as his companion, as a constant presence in his young life, William felt at ease.

Unfortunately, after a few years, Diana, who had been supportive of her sisterly relationship with William and Harry, changed her opinion of Tiggy. The problems began when the boys would return home to the palace; they would talk nonstop about what they had done with Tiggy, and Diana began to feel jealous and left out. As well, she and Tiggy had differing opinions about how the boys should be raised. For her part, Tiggy felt that the boys should behave as young adults, and with Charles's blessing, she saw to it that they received whatever they wanted. Diana began to disassociate the boys from Tiggy, in effect freezing her out of their lives as much as possible. When this happened, William did not understand and felt as if his loyalties were being tested. There was no doubt that he deeply loved his mother, yet he felt love for Tiggy too and did not want to choose between them. It was not long before he learned to keep tales of the happy times to himself. Despite Diana's feelings, Tiggy was an important part of William's life for years to come, and her influence continued throughout his formative years. When she left Charles's employ and married many years later, William was a guest at her wedding.

THE WELL-TRAVELED BOY

Throughout his young life, William traveled extensively. From his first trip to Australia when he was just a few weeks old to trips during his school recesses and on holidays, William and the Royal Family traveled to exclusive and luxurious places about which commoners could only dream. During summer holidays in 1986 and 1987, and in 1988 and 1990, William and the Royal Family spent time with members of Spain's Royal Family in Majorca. In May 1988, William and Harry, along with their nanny and a bodyguard, visited the Scilly Isles, and they returned there the next year. In January 1989 and in April 1990, William, Harry, and Diana went on holiday to the Virgin Islands and stayed on Necker Island, owned by businessman Sir Richard Branson. And during the summer of 1989, William, with his bodyguard in tow, went to Portugal with a school friend. Although these trips seemed exotic and carefree to most people, more typical holiday destinations are not available to the likes of Prince William and the Royal Family; for sure, spontaneity in travel is not enjoyed by the famous, the rich, or certainly, any members of the Royal Family and the heir to the British throne.

THE IDOL OF MILLIONS OF BRITISH TEENAGE GIRLS—THE RISE OF "WILLY MANIA"

In Britain, to be deemed "poster-perfect" for teen magazines, a young man must possess three essential attributes: wealth, fame, and what the British people call snogability—what makes teenage girls hyperventilate. Although it is usually rock stars and actors who have these attributes, when William turned 14, he too possessed these qualities and appeared in the October 1996 edition of the teen publication *Smash Hits*. Inside the magazine, which became a top seller, was a pullout of William wearing a blue sports jacket. The May 1996 issue of the same magazine, which sold approximately 250,000 copies, contained "I Love Willy" stickers. The British newspaper *The Sun* declared William a "smasher," or a seriously adorable guy. Another teen magazine, *Live & Kicking*, included a top 10 list of reasons Prince William was cool. The list included the following: "He knows how to partee! He wears trainers [sneakers] instead of sensible shoes" and "He's not scared of going on scary theme park rides." The editor of the magazine, Jeremy Mark, concluded, "Our readers have latched onto the fact that he's the same age as they are and has the same interest. This is the first time a member of the Royal Family has been popular with teenagers. They see him as a regular boy growing up in Britain."

In October 1996, William arrived at London's Hammersmith Palais nightclub, along with two Scotland Yard detectives, for his first teenage dance. With his friends fending off girls who wanted to introduce themselves to the future king, William spent the night dancing and waving his arms in the air to the music; knowing the press was watching, he was always mindful of what he was doing and where he was.[12]

A SMALL AMOUNT OF FREEDOM—WILLIAM LEARNS TO DRIVE

Learning to drive and getting a car provides most young men a certain amount of freedom and independence, and for William, any sort of freedom was welcomed in his tightly controlled and narrow royal world. It was in the summer of 1999 that William learned to drive. Driving a car also enabled William at 17 years of age to satisfy his wish for fast travel. Of course, his driving always took place with a police bodyguard in the passenger seat or following close behind in an unmarked car, so there was little possibility that William could drive too fast. An interest in driving fast came early for this teen; when he was much younger, he and Diana had enjoyed going go-karting, and he loved riding a quad-bike around the Queen's estate at Balmoral. William also loved motorbikes and even took a motorcycle maintenance course while studying at Eton College. He could be seen riding around on the roads in the Cotswolds on a motorbike, wearing a helmet and a visor, when he was 16 years old. As soon as he was 17, the legal driving age in Britain, William began his driving lessons. On his 17th birthday, Charles gave William a used Volkswagen Golf GTI. Once he had his provisional driver's license, he showed off his new driving skills for the media by driving in front of Highgrove Estate, stopping just short of the cameras and the gathered reporters. William passed the driving test in July 1999, just five weeks after his 17th birthday.

As in previous years and on other birthdays, William once again declined to give a media interview. He did, however, agree to complete a questionnaire, where he said he enjoyed casual clothes, dance and pop music, and driving a car. He also noted that team sports including water polo, football, and rugby were his forte and that in his spare time he enjoyed being with his friends, going to see action movies, and watching football and rugby matches. He also said he wanted to be a private person away from the public and media spotlight: "I don't like attention. I feel uncomfortable with it. But I have particularly appreciated being left alone at Eton, which has allowed me to concentrate on my school work and enjoy being with my friends without being followed by camera. I am grateful to the media for helping to protect my privacy and I hope I can enjoy the same freedom at university."[13]

THE ROYAL PRINCE TURNS 18

William turned 18 on June 21, 2000, and the world was getting a clearer look at the young man who would someday be king. He was in his final year at Eton College, and as a wildly popular teen, he was captain of the swim team, he earned the school cadet corps' top honors, and he competed in polo and soccer. As a top student at the prestigious Eton, he studied art history, geography, and biology, and he was a prefect, one of the elected elite students with disciplinary duties; he wore the prefect uniform of checked pants, bow tie, and colorful waistcoat. Blending in at school, or anywhere for that matter, was not an option for William. Certainly, he was the future king, which in and of itself made him stand out; however, he was also quite handsome, and at 6'2" tall, he had his mother's stunning blue eyes. William was voted Britain's most eligible single man in 1999 in *Tatler* magazine, which called him a "future king who . . . enjoys boating and the odd party or two."[14]

At 18, William received an official coat of arms that had been authorized by the Queen. He had helped design the crest, which incorporated an emblem from his mother's family's coat of arms; the crest featured a lion and unicorn on either side of the shield, topped by a coronet and a second, smaller lion, and also featured a small, red scallop from the Spencer coat of arms. The scallop appeared four times in the middle point of four three-pointed white collars around the lion, unicorn, and shield. The collars or labels, as they are called, are used only in arms of the sovereign's children or the eldest son of the Prince of Wales.[15]

At 18 years of age, William was now on his way to being a thoughtful, somewhat shy, intelligent, sensitive, and thoroughly modern monarch.

NOTES

1. Brian Hoey, *Prince William* (Phoenix Mill, England: Sutton, 2003), 35.

2. Ibid., 41.

3. Tim Graham and Peter Archer, *William: HRH Prince William of Wales* (New York: Atria Books, 2003), 20.

4. Michelle Green, "A Royal First," *People Weekly*, June 27, 1983, 89+.

5. Ibid.

6. Tim Graham and Peter Archer, *William: HRH Prince William of Wales* (New York: Atria Books, 2003), 43.

7. Brian Hoey, *Prince William* (Phoenix Mill, England: Sutton, 2003), 47–48.

8. Tim Graham and Peter Archer, *William: HRH Prince William of Wales* (New York: Atria Books, 2003), 52.

9. Fred Bernstein, "William the Terrible; Di's Darling Is a Precocious Tot Who Can Be a Royal Pain," *People Weekly*, July 7, 1986, 106+.

10. Ibid.

11. Brian Hoey, *Prince William* (Phoenix Mill, England: Sutton, 2003), 49, 52.

12. Janice Min, "Prince Dreamboat," *People Weekly*, July 1, 1996, 72+.

13. Ibid., 126, 128.

14. "Prince Charming: Sporty, Swoon-Worthy and Strikingly Sensible as They Approach Adulthood, William and Harry Do Both Their Parents Proud," *People Weekly*, April 24, 2000, 98+.

15. Tim Graham and Peter Archer, *William: HRH Prince William of Wales* (New York: Atria Books, 2003), 124, 126.

Chapter 3

THE PRINCE'S EDUCATION

In the early history of the monarchy, most royal children were educated in the royal palace. In more recent history, it became the tradition that children were sent to boarding schools. Just a few months after turning eight, William was enrolled at the Ludgrove School, a boarding school in Berkshire. He studied there for five years. For Diana, sending William away to board at a preparatory school was a very difficult decision. For Charles, following tradition was very important; however, because his own experience at prep school had been somewhat difficult, he was sensitive to what many young boys experience while attending boarding school, and he wanted William's experience to be positive. Just as careful thought had been given to where young William would go to nursery school, so was the choice of the appropriate boarding school carefully considered. After much consideration, it was decided that the Ludgrove School was the best possible choice for William. Charles and Diana were impressed by its facilities, its well-known, rigorous academic program, and the pastoral care provided to the pupils. Of course, having a royal attend the school called for some changes. The school and the students, including the young prince, were now protected by new fencing, reinforced glass, and video cameras. As well, William's personal protection officer was installed in a room next to William's room; he was advised not to interfere with William and his friends, but to remain in the background as much as possible. For further security, William had a buzzer beside his bed and another to be worn on his wrist at all times.

Accompanied by both parents, William arrived at the school on the morning of September 10, 1990. Met by the headmasters, William was a composed eight-year-old, but his mother was clearly in tears. Once his parents left, William became homesick, not unlike many of his classmates, but he soon settled into the school's routines. He sent letters home to his mother, who treasured them, and also received many letters from her, addressed to "My Darling Wombat." William later said that his years at Ludgrove were some of the happiest in his life; however, initially the time appeared to be difficult for the young prince. He was often described as a serious youngster, quite shy, certainly intelligent, and quite self-possessed for a boy his age. The high-spirited nature of his younger years was seemingly gone; it was as if his parents' marital problems, still publicly denied but certainly evident to William, had taken a toll on a youngster who had been so often spontaneous and full of spirit. He sometimes seemed burdened with worry and was often seen walking by himself on the remote school grounds, his shoulders hunched, looking as if he was deep in thought. Through it all, he applied himself to his studies and quickly showed his abilities in English; in the summer of 1992, he won the Junior Essay Prize. His interest in geography also blossomed, and he maintained the interest throughout his academic life. It was also during his early years at Ludgrove that his caring nature and social conscience became evident. As part of his studies, he often participated in volunteer and charitable programs. He had a developing interest in the disadvantaged and the aged population in the area. In May 1994 and 1995, he participated in sponsored walks for the Workingham District Association for the Elderly.

By the time he entered Ludgrove, William was taller than most of the classmates his age. And it was not long after settling in that his interest in sports and his athletic skills were sharpened. He participated in several sports throughout the year: he played basketball, was the captain of his rugby and hockey teams, and was a top competitor in clay pigeon shooting. Participation in athletic activities often provides its own set of perils for young people, and for William, it was no different. On June

3, 1991, at a Ludgrove-sponsored sporting event, William was hit by a golf club while playing with a friend on the school's putting green. He was quickly sent to the Royal Berkshire Hospital in Reading, suffering a depressed fracture of the forehead; fortunately, he was not knocked out. He was shortly transferred by ambulance to London's Great Ormond Street Hospital for Sick Children and underwent an operation to relieve the pressure in his skull. While he was at the hospital, Diana refused to leave his side until she was convinced he was out of danger.

While William was at Ludgrove, Charles and Diana often visited him, and despite their royal status and busy schedules and responsibilities, they readily took part in student and parent activities. Even though he felt somewhat embarrassed by his parents' obvious notoriety, and had typical adolescent self-consciousness, the times his parents visited and took part in various school activities were very special. In June 1995, William and his father participated in the school's father-and-son clay pigeon shooting competition. In July 1995, he and Diana played in the mother-and-son tennis competition, and although the two did not win their match, observers noted that it was quite evident that winning did not matter. Although Charles and Diana had always been very much involved in both William and Harry's life, their own relationship had steadily deteriorated over the years, and the tensions between them were nearly always evident, though Buckingham Palace continued to deny any troubles. When they were together, Charles and Diana were often fighting, and it was difficult for their sensitive eldest son to cope. However, he did cherish his time with each of them.

THE ROYAL PARENTS' PUBLIC SEPARATION

When William enrolled as a student at Ludgrove, he arrived with the weight of his parents' obvious marriage difficulties on his mind; in 1995, he left Ludgrove as a casualty of their separation and eventual divorce. Charles and Diana's wedding had been the fairy tale of the century. Unfortunately, their marriage was often described as a roller coaster ride. The births of William and Harry were certainly deemed as two of their marital successes, and the births were pointed to as a sign of marital bliss. But almost from the beginning, Diana was unhappy and showed signs of stress. It was not long after Harry was born in 1984 that Diana's life within the palace walls was beginning to crumble. Some said she suffered from postpartum depression and described her suffering as feeling trapped. The fights became regular, and increasingly, Charles and Diana led separate lives. By 1987, when William was just five, signs of a break in the marriage were causing speculation in the media. Diana was sure that Charles was spending time with his longtime love, Camilla Parker Bowles, and she began to spend time with an old friend herself. In March 1991, her relationship with a cavalry officer became public knowledge. The marriage crisis came to a head in 1992 when a former royal biographer published a book that claimed the marriage had been a charade; Diana had stated she was living within a loveless marriage, and it was revealed she was suffering from an eating disorder; a rumor circulated that she had threatened to kill herself. A formal separation seemed inevitable.

The marital difficulties and subsequent separation were kept out of the media as much and as long as possible and were continually publicly denied by Buckingham Palace until December 1992, when William was 10 and Harry was 8. Before the announcement was made, Diana visited William and Harry at Ludgrove to break the news to them. The two boys took the news differently. For William, it was devastating, and he broke down in tears. Harry did not seem to understand what his mother was saying; he was quite bewildered by the news. After two years of separation and continued bickering, Charles and Diana had finally reached an amicable understanding.

Although being a royal has obvious privileges and benefits, the Royals could always count on being in the public eye, like or not. As William grew older, he often resented this continued spotlight and living within the constant glare of the media, especially when it came to his mother and father's relationship. Even before the breakup of their marriage became public knowledge, Charles and Diana were always at the forefront of the media, and their pictures were, more often than not, splashed on the front page of every kind of newspaper. As a boy, William was always shielded from the tabloid newspapers, and he rarely watched television or listened to the radio in an effort to avoid stories about his family. Charles and Diana's decision to separate was announced in the House of Commons by Prime Minister John Major in early December 1992. Mr. Major, speaking to a quiet House of Commons, insisted that there were no constitutional implications arising from the royal separation and there would not be a divorce. Of course, he related nothing about the certain, inevitable impact on the lives of the two boys, both in line to be the sovereign king.

Once his parents separated, William spent his time outside of school with Diana at Kensington Palace in London and with Charles at Highgrove House in Gloucestershire, his estate not far from London. Although there were trips with either the Prince or the Princess, they were rarely ever again together as a family. For years, the only thing that had seemed to keep Charles and Diana together was William and Harry. After the separation, it seemed that the only thing keeping the two from divorce was also their two boys.

A YOUNG ROYAL "ETONIAN"

William finished his education at the Ludgrove School in 1995. Just like his father before him, decisions regarding upbringing and certainly his formal education were made with an eye toward his someday being king. Decisions regarding how William would be educated early in his life were part tradition and part a departure from such traditions in comparison to past royals, but the fact remained that his upbringing and education were part of his training. William had very little control over his future or in the paths he would take toward that future. The next step for his education, after Ludgrove, was to attend Eton College, a prestigious school for boys, located in Berkshire, just across the river Thames from Windsor Castle. In England, students attend what is known as college from the ages of 13 through 18; this can be compared to junior high and high school in the U.S. For William, although he may have been asked if he wanted to attend Eton College, there was very little chance that his desire not to attend the school would be considered. As expected, in June 1995, word came from the palace that William had passed the entrance examination for one of England's most prestigious schools, Eton College.

As it happened, the decision to attend Eton was a very good and happy one for William, given that many of his school friends from Ludgrove were also attending the school. However, his grandfather, Prince Philip, was said to have been disappointed that William was not attending Gordonstoun, the Scottish school he and his three sons,

*Britain's Prince Charles, right, and his estranged
wife Princess Diana, second from left, flank their
children, Harry, third from right, and William, at
Eton College, west of London, September 6, 1995.
Prince William, heir to the throne, arrived for his
first day at the school, which has for more than 500
years educated the sons of Britain's elite. Prince
William's new house master, Dr. Andrew Gailey,
stands at far left. (AP Photo/Lynne Sladky)*

including Prince Charles, William's father, had attended. But Charles's
time at that school had been difficult. The school was known for, during
Charles's time there at least, its austere regime of cold baths and early
morning cross-country runs. Charles was pleased when Diana and the
Queen suggested William attend Eton, one of the most famous and
prestigious schools in the world. Diana was said to have always wanted
both her sons to attend this prominent school, and she was instrumen-
tal in the choice. She wanted William to follow in the footsteps of her
"Old Etonian" father, Earl Spencer, and her brother, Charles Spencer.
For the Queen, it was an excellent choice for William, partly because

it was so close to Windsor Castle and also because she could keep her eye on him there. During William's time at Eton, he often visited the Queen at Windsor Castle, taking afternoon tea with her. Chris Patten, a former minister of education and an old friend of Prince Charles, and someone not involved in the initial decision to send William to Eton, stated he had no doubt that Eton was the best option for the young prince: "It's an outstanding school. It produces young men who have self-confidence . . . and instills charm that is an admirable mix of wit, scholarship . . . the boys who go there are an amazing mix of types and cultures, races and religions . . . Eton is a school that offers something for everyone: tradition, discipline and discretions."[1]

Eton College, often referred to simply as Eton, is an independent boarding school for boys ages 13 to 18. Founded in 1440 by King Henry VI as "the King's College of Our Lady of Eton besides Wyndsor," it is located in the town of Eton, which is near the town of Windsor and Windsor Castle. In attending Eton, William was certainly in good company; the school has an extensive list of distinguished former pupils including prime ministers, poets, political leaders, novelists, war heroes, philosophers, and countless other royals. The school, in the more recent past, also has boasted of students who are the sons of rock stars and business moguls. Eton is known as the school where the children of the nation's elite have been educated for centuries. Still an all-boys school, the college's official Web site states, "Eton has educated boys for nearly six centuries. The College continues to develop Henry VI's original vision by providing a distinctive education, which we aim to make accessible to any talented boy."[2] Even though Eton was established nearly six centuries ago, it has a modern curriculum with high academic standards and opportunities that include sports, drama, music, and the arts. On the historic campus, there are three theaters, two concert halls, and two noteworthy libraries. Although the boarding halls are considered ancient by today's standards, they are constantly updated with the latest technology. For the students at Eton, including young William, who entered in September 1995, the school's educational aims include

> promoting the best habits of independent thought and learning in the pursuit of excellence; providing a broadly-based education designed to enable all boys to discover their strengths, and

to make the most of their talents within Eton and beyond; en-
gendering respect for individuality, difference, the importance
of teamwork and the contribution that each boy makes to the
life of the school and the community; supporting pastoral care
that nurtures physical health, emotional maturity and spiritual
richness; and fostering self-confidence, enthusiasm, perseverance,
tolerance and integrity.[3]

To be sure, William's time at Eton was disciplined, educational, and
academically rigorous, at a place known for its strictness and traditions
and as a safe place for a modern royal to learn and live.

In September 1995, when William was just 13 years old, he arrived
at Eton dressed in a tweed jacket, grey trousers, and a tie. He was accompanied by his parents and his brother, who would also enroll at
the school two years later. A few days earlier, he and Diana had attended the new boys' luncheon at Manor House, which would be his
new home while at the school. There he had met his classmates and
was shown about the House and the school. His room was just like the
other boys' rooms, except that he personalized it and made it his own.
Of course, there was one notable difference between William and the
other boys; he was guarded day and night and was always accompanied by his personal police officer, who had a room close by. Luckily,
the man appointed to guard William was married with two sons of his
own, so he knew about boys William's age, and he was aware of how
much freedom William needed and wanted. If William strolled into
town with his friend, walked about the school grounds, or visited a
shop, there were always police officers dressed in suits, with their guns
beneath their jackets, discreetly about, keeping a safe, tactful distance.
Although there were other boys at Eton from famous families, William
certainly stood out, and most did their best to ignore both William's
fame and his bodyguards. The school, the town of Eton, and the nearby
town of Windsor are all havens for tourists, and there is no way to cor-
don off the area to protect an heir to the throne; keeping William safe
was not the easiest of tasks.

In addition to being watched by his bodyguards, William was also
always watched by the media. As with other royals throughout recent
history at least, the media was a constant presence. However, for this

royal, the public remained more than just interested, and the media was more than merely present. With his shy good looks and resemblance to his famous mother, with his parents in the midst of a much-publicized separation, and with his father the next in line to be king, William had always had the media around him, and when he arrived at Eton, the media was present to record every event as the young, popular prince entered the hallowed halls of a deeply traditional, prestigious college. However, just as in the past, there was a tacit agreement with media editors that pictures and stories would be provided to the press at significant events in William's life, in return for their allowing William his privacy while in school. Editors agreed not to send their staff to disturb William or any of the school's staff or students or to buy freelance photos of William, thus halting the paparazzi from constantly being present, for William's sake and for the sake of the other boys at the school.

William was assigned to board in Manor House, one of the oldest sites on the campus, where he would live for the next five years. A portrait of the Duke of Wellington hung in the main hall of the house, a reminder to young William of the deep-seated tradition and history of the school that he was now a part of. Such traditions and historical significance were essentially a part of his very being, and as a result, these kinds of reminders were commonplace, yet certainly important to the teen prince. Manor House was the center of William's world, a place where he slept, ate, and studied, and most of the sports that he participated in were played in the house's colors of beige and blue. Although he was the only boy at Eton to have a private bathroom, his room was typical of other English schools, and William decorated it to fit his style. Above his narrow single bed, he pinned an autographed poster of his favorite band, All Saints, and when he was a bit older, he added a poster of the supermodel Cindy Crawford and another of tennis star Anna Kournikova. Displayed on his dressing table was an empty bottle of Grand Vin de Chateau Latour, vintage 1966, the year England won the World Cup. On his desk were two photographs, one of his mother wearing a red jacket and the other a full-length portrait of his father in a Guards uniform. Just like the other boys at Eton, William was required to don the regulation uniform of black tailcoat, waistcoat, striped trousers, and a white bow tie; this traditional uniform dates back to the death of King George III in 1820, when the college was in mourning for His Majesty the King.

On the day after his arrival, William attended his first lesson dressed in the school's distinctive uniform. One of his first duties was to learn to speak in the language of the school, a new language to William and the nine other new boys in Manor House. For instance, teachers were "beaks," lessons were "schools," and homework was referred to as "EWs" or "extra work." Each school term was called a "half" despite there being three a year, a practice that dates from the 16th century when there were only two terms per year.[4] Eton is unique among British schools in that the curriculum not only includes the typical academic subjects and classical languages such as Greek and Latin but also offers courses in Mandarin Chinese, Japanese, Arabic, and some nontraditional subjects such as auto mechanics and cooking. Initially, William studied English, Latin, French, geography, history, divinity, math, the sciences, and art and music; he also participated in physical education and had gym classes. As expected, he performed exceptionally well in his studies and on his General Certificate of Secondary Education (GCSE) exam. On the exam, generally taken in a number of subjects by students ages 14–16, William earned "A-star" scores in Latin and French in 1997; and the following year, he earned an "A-star" in biology and A's in English, English literature, geography, history, and Spanish. He earned B's in math and French.[5] William's last two years at Eton were spent preparing to enter university. He concentrated his coursework in the history of art, which included trips to London art galleries, the Tate Museum, the Victoria and Albert Museum, the Royal Academy, and the National Gallery. He also did further study in geography that included trips to Oxfordshire, England, the London Docklands, Dartmoor, and northeast England, as well as lectures at the Royal Society. He joined the Combined Cadet Corps, which gives boys basic military training, and was also a member of the winning drill syndicate at a military-style parade held in December 1998. William was a part of the Eton Tattoo in June 1999, and he won the Sword of Honour as the top first-year cadet. William's success as a part of the cadet corps allowed for speculation that he would follow in many of his ancestors' footsteps and serve in the armed forces.

William excelled academically at Eton, and he also continued to hone his skills in various sports, just as he had done at Ludgrove. At Eton, he focused on his swimming skills. As a junior, he won the 50-meter and 100-meter titles, and as a senior, he captained the school swimming team. During the term, he swam every day, and while at Buckingham Palace, he used the pool there, where he preferred to swim alone, rather than with other members of the family, unlike his mother, who would use the pool often and invite other members of the family or the household staff to join her.

At Eton, religious instruction is stressed for all boys, and depending on personal faith, all boys were required to attend chapel every day. Although the school accepts students of all faiths, it is predominantly Christian in its teaching. The prospectus informs all parents of pupils that "Eton College was founded . . . for the worship of God and for the training of young men to the service of the Church and State."[6] This was one of the reasons that the late Queen Mother, Queen Mary, was strongly insistent on William attending Eton, and why the Queen and Prince Charles readily agreed. It is perhaps the perfect school for a future king to learn the basic facts of the Church, over which, as sovereign, he will be the supreme governor. If William would have any doubts about the spiritual aspects of his future role, he could refer to the founder of Eton and one of his ancestors, Henry VI, whose life was devoted to prayer and to service.

With all of his achievements at Eton, young William was deemed to be one of the most academic members of the Windsor family, and he was considered destined for great achievements when he went on to university. However, all of William's academic success came in the midst of his personal heartaches. By the time he arrived at Eton, his parents had separated, and although he was ready to attend the prestigious school, he was also an unhappy 13-year-old as a result of his parents' strained and difficult relationship. Within a year, in August 1996, Charles and Diana were divorced after a 15-year marriage, but luckily for William, his friends did not care about the divorce and were supportive of their friend and classmate. Royalty had been a part of Eton for many years, and the fact that William was a child of divorced parents made him one of the many instead of one of the few; there was nothing seemingly new or unusual about parents breaking up. However, for William, the airing of dirty laundry was problematic and made life much more difficult, especially for such a sensitive young man. In November 1995, Diana told a television audience of her infidelity with a cavalryman who had taught William polo skills. In the same interview, Diana blamed Camilla Parker Bowles, Charles's longtime love, for the breakdown of her and Charles's marriage and even questioned whether Charles was suited to be the next king.

William had grown up amid his parents' marital problems, yet he remained traumatized by their breakup. He did wish for both his parents to be happier, hoped they would at least be friends, and wished for a brighter future for himself and for both of them. In March 1997, his parents were reunited for one of the last times when William was confirmed at St. George's Chapel, Windsor, by the Bishop of London. Attending the service were both Charles and Diana and other members of the Royal Family, and although his parents were no longer married, they did seem to be at least civil to each other. In early June of that year, William made a rather brave decision and asked his parents to not attend the parents' day activities at Eton, feeling their attendance, and that of the media, which were surely to attend in full force, would be too disruptive for the students and the activities. Instead, he invited his former nanny, Tiggy Legge-Bourke, and another good friend, William van Cutsem, to attend. Without his parents there, William seemed to be far more at ease, smiling and enjoying the activities.

Later that same month, it was William's idea for Diana and him to attend a charity auction in New York, where he also suggested Diana donate some of her formal dresses to be auctioned to support various charities. The sale of the gowns netted more than 2 million pounds, and Diana gave young William the credit for the idea and the donation.

Although William enjoyed his five years at Eton and excelled in his studies and in sports, the same five years involved great turmoil in the Royal Family. Divorces and scandals brought the monarchy to its lowest point in the esteem of the English people, and until Diana's death in 1997, the reputation of the Royals was at its lowest point ever. William was, however, safe, seemingly unscathed, and out of the news of the Royal Family that permeated the media; at Eton, he was sheltered, and it proved to be the perfect place for him to be during a very difficult time, both personally and for the Royal Family as a whole. William said of the media at the time, "I don't like the attention. I feel uncomfortable with it, but I have particularly appreciated being left alone at Eton, which has allowed me to concentrate on my school work and enjoy being with my friends without being followed by cameras."[7]

WILLIAM'S GAP YEAR

William finished his education at Eton in June 2000. He had worked hard in his studies, and he could have gone straight to university; however, with his father's blessing, he decided to take a year off, or in English parlance, take a "gap" year. He engaged in a great amount of planning in deciding where he would go and what he would do. Chris Patten, the former minister of education and an old friend of Prince Charles, noted that a gap year should have elements of travel, include adventure, and have an educational aspect. He thought that the travel should be to an exotic place, that adding a somewhat dangerous element to the adventure would make it more exciting, and that because it was part of the educational process for any student, and especially for one destined to be king, it should be educational.[8]

Charles decided that William should gain experience in service, and William spent the first part of the gap year in the jungles of Belize. In 2000, William spent a week with 40 British Commandos and stated later that it was the most difficult week of his life. Not asking for any special treatment, he lived in the same quarters as the military personnel, including a hammock strung between two trees to sleep in. William's training did not include killing a pig, as others commandos were taught to do; however, he did have to use a machete to kill and gut a chicken and then cook it over an open fire to feed the troops. William was used to hunting and shooting outings with his family at Windsor, Balmoral, Sandringham, and other royal properties and as a result was an excellent shot with hunting firearms, but he had never handled military-style semiautomatic weapons; during his week in Belize, he learned to use them and was described as being an excellent marksman. Upon his return to England, with his father by his side, William held a press conference where he detailed his experiences in Belize, playing down his experiences in the jungle, including an illness from insects, reptiles, and other dangers that all the commandos face as part of their training.

In the second part of his gap-year experience, he joined the Royal Geographical Society in a program called Shoals of Capricorn, a course that teaches marine conservation. William traveled to the island of Rodrigues, located approximately 300 miles southeast of Mauritius in the Indian Ocean. On this trip, William found an island entirely different from Belize. Rodrigues had empty white beaches, palm trees, and cool breezes, and it was utterly peaceful there. He stayed in a small village lodge, and the local population did not know who was actually in their midst. William drove about the island on a rented Honda moped, hoping to teach the local fisherman how damaging their practice of using dynamite to blow the fish to the surface and then collecting their catch was; unfortunately, his advice on how else fish could be caught and sold did not meet with success. During his stay on the island, he also scuba dived to inspect the coral reefs for environmental damage, and in his off-duty time, he taught young men how to play rugby.

While at Eton, William had met many new people and made many new friends, yet most of them were from wealthy families. As part of his education, it was deemed important that he develop relationships with all kinds of people from around the world; thus, the next part of William's year of education before university was to join an overseas expedition to gain experience with other people his own age from around the world and from other walks of life. For many years, Charles had been a supporter of Raleigh International, including as a supporter of its original expedition in 1984. The organization, according to its Web site, is

a leading youth and education charity and since 1984 our expeditions have inspired over 30,000 people from all walks of life, nationalities and ages to be all they can be, helping them develop new skills, friendships and volunteer to make a genuine difference to communities and environments across the world . . . as a charity our goal isn't just to make the most of your volunteering experience but also to ensure our projects deliver long term sustainable benefits in the communities and environments we work with.[9]

The organization's goal was exactly what Charles wanted for his eldest son, and he was confident that the resulting experience would broaden William's views and serve him well in his future. Before William could join an expedition, he had to gain sponsorships to pay for the trip, so he organized and played in a polo match; Charles matched the money raised as a contribution to the organization to assist disadvantaged youth who wished to join the expedition.

William had a choice of an expedition to Mongolia, Namibia, Ghana, or Chile; he chose Chile, and the palace approved his choice. He had been curious about the country but had never visited, and he felt that living in a remote area of the country would help him learn more about himself and help others. Also, he was determined to get away from the media spotlight and insisted that no one accompany him on the trip, except of course his personal police officer who had constant contact with the palace through a satellite phone. William worked with more than 100 other volunteers from varied backgrounds on environmental and community projects, including improving local buildings and constructing walkways. The first part of his stay was truly a test of his stamina. He said upon his return to England that the weather and the terrain in the hills of Patagonia were difficult at best and that at first, it was wet, cold, and miserable. Everyone was completely wet through, and the food was appalling, at least in part because they were not able to build fires to have hot meals. However, neither William nor the men and women on the expedition considered giving up. After the first week, the weather cleared, and everyone was able to get to work. William taught the village children English, constructed buildings for the village, and had a hand in whatever needed to done. He lived in a shack, slept in a tent, chopped wood, cooked meals, scrubbed floors, and just like the other volunteers, cleaned toilets. He said at the time, "The living conditions here aren't exactly what I'm used to . . . you don't have any secrets. You share everything with everyone. I found it very difficult myself to start with because I am a very private person. But I learnt to deal with it." One of the other volunteers described William as laid-back and easygoing; he said that William got along well with everyone else, whatever their backgrounds, and that he earned the respect of the volunteers and staff and was very well liked. He added that

William was popular not because of who he was, but because of what he accomplished, and that he was "completely human and normal and one of the gang."[10]

William returned home for Christmas, and in the early months of 2001, he worked on a dairy farm in southwest England where he rose before dawn to milk cows and muck out the barns. He spent the final part of his gap year in Africa, where for three months he traveled to several countries on safari and worked on game conservation issues. William's gap year was everything he and his father had hoped it would be. He broadened his outlook; worked hard in difficult, challenging environments; met people from all walks of life and from all types of status and backgrounds; and made new friends. He also, through all the hard work, became more muscular and fit. Learning about other cultures, helping others, enduring difficult and demanding environments, and being away from the confines of the palace, of castles, of the Royal Family, and even of school all proved to be beneficial to the young prince and likely helped him in his education and training geared toward someday becoming the sovereign king.

ON TO THE UNIVERSITY OF ST. ANDREWS

The next step in the prince's life was to further his education and move to Scotland to attend the University of St. Andrews to study art history. Located approximately 50 miles from Edinburgh, on the east coast of Scotland, St. Andrews is Scotland's first university and the third oldest in the English-speaking world. It was founded in 1413, and over six centuries, it has established a reputation as one of Europe's leading and most distinctive centers for teaching and research.[11] Although William was given a say in which university he would attend, the choice was made after a group of individuals that included the Bishop of London, a senior army officer, and Chris Patten (as mentioned previously, Charles's old friend and former minister of education) made a recommendation to Charles. For his part, Charles wanted to give the best advice possible to his son, and he was determined that a decision would not be imposed on William without his agreement or without consideration of William's interests and ambitions. When it was disclosed where William would further his studies, he was asked what he was most looking forward to; he stated he wanted to be able to manage his own time in a relaxed atmosphere and have more independence, although, he added, having a policeman around all the time meant he would never be alone or truly independent.

Before William moved to St. Andrews in 2001, the Queen set certain rules, including that there would be no smoking, only moderate drinking, and definitely no drugs; also, if he was to go on a date, he was not to be seen kissing her in public, to never attempt to rid himself of his personal police protection, and to never discuss any member of the Royal Family with anyone. Before he arrived at St. Andrews, William gave an official interview in which he stated, "People who try to take advantage of me and get a piece of me, I spot quickly and soon go off them." Although William had practice with the media and with individuals who attempted to take advantage of him and his status, his abilities and wit were quickly tested. While he was enjoying friends at a local bar, a passing coed patted William on the posterior. William quickly gave her a look of sharp disdain, and another student noted that William was not impressed by such behavior. Such behaviors often presented dilemmas for the prince as he tried to maintain a balance between being a college student and a part of typical student activities and having his own anonymity while being famous and the future heir to the throne. According to Peter Archer, Britain's Press Association royals correspondent, the issue of how William would best fit in when he clearly stood out was difficult, and William remained an extremely shy, private young man when he first attended university. Archer noted, "He is very conscious of being exploited and wants to avoid it. He thinks his mother is still being exploited, and a lot of his actions are based on what happened to Diana."[12] Going by the name William Wales, rather than the Prince or being addressed as "Sir," William tried very hard to live like other students. He shopped at the local supermarket, he attended lectures with as many as 200 other students, and he spent the evenings reading or with his friends, enjoying pints of beer at pubs near campus.

After William enrolled at St. Andrews, there was an increase in the number of applications for acceptance at the school. The residents of the small town were aware of having such a well-known student among them. Local businesses benefited from an increase in tourism, and property values and prices increased. While the media invaded the town and swarmed the campus, everyone was protective of the prince in their midst and refused to provide any information or details about where William was or what he did. Although the town benefited from William's attendance at St. Andrews, there were some drawbacks for the students. The tradition of grades posted on university bulletin boards ended, there were additional security cameras installed around campus, and the extra police presence was noted by all students. What was normal for William took some getting used to for his fellow students.

As is tradition at the beginning of the term, all students are given an older student to advise them about the school. Among William's advisors was an American student who was the granddaughter of a former member of the Queen's household. Another advisor was a former Eton student, like William. Both the palace and the school denied they had anything to do with either of these appointments and said that they were not handpicked for William.

William said he hoped to make many new friends from a broad cross-section of students at St. Andrews and not just remain within a circle of aristocrats and students from wealthy families, known as "yahs" by the rest of the students not of this circle, who make up about 60 percent of the 6,500 students at the school. He said, "It's not as if I choose my friends on the basis of where they are from or what they are. It's about their character and who they are and whether we get on. I just hope I can meet people I get on with. I don't care about backgrounds." He also hoped to have lively debates with anti-monarchists at the school and stated, "To me, someone can hold a view about something without it making a difference to who they are. Everyone has opinions and they are entitled to them. I can still get on with them, even if I don't agree with what they might believe."[13]

William lived in a residence hall for the first two years and then decided it was time for him to move out, which took a great deal of preparation and planning for the palace. Of course, it was not simply a matter of finding a place and moving in; security police had to inspect the property and check the backgrounds of fellow student roommates. They also alerted neighbors of the likely disruptions that would accompany having the prince nearby and also ensured that the local police station was close by in case they were needed. By William's third year at

St. Andrews, there were noticeable changes, including a continued rise in applications, a resulting hike in academic standards, and a challenging social cachet that included overcoming barriers put up by William and his friends against those who might sell stories to the tabloids, who seemed to be always nearby. Fortunately, William did find his fellow students and the school itself to be fiercely loyal and protective of his privacy.

When William entered St. Andrews, he originally planned to major art history. He changed his major to geography and wrote his final dissertation on a study of the coral reefs of Rodrigues in the Indian Ocean, where he had spent time during his gap year. Also as part of his geography studies, he traveled to Norway to see the Jostedalen ice cap, the largest in mainland Europe. In June 2005, the palace announced that William had received a 2:1 (honors) degree in geography. He graduated from St. Andrews on June 23, 2005. The Queen; her husband, the Duke of Edinburgh; and the Duke and Duchess of Rothesay (William's father and stepmother, also known as the Prince of Wales and the Duchess of Cornwall) attended the graduation ceremony.[14]

NOTES

1. Brian Hoey, *Prince William* (Phoenix Mill, England: Sutton, 2003), 75–76.

2. Eton College Web Site, http://www.etoncollege.com (accessed May 11, 2010).

3. Ibid. (accessed May 13, 2010).

4. Tim Graham and Peter Archer, *William HRH Prince William of Wales* (New York: Atria Books, 2003), 104.

5. Ibid., 106.

6. Brian Hoey, *Prince William* (Phoenix Mill, England: Sutton, 2003), 85.

7. Tim Graham and Peter Archer, *William HRH Prince William of Wales* (New York: Atria Books, 2003), 109.

8. Brian Hoey, *Prince William* (Phoenix Mill, England: Sutton, 2003), 88.

9. Raleigh Web Site, http://www.raleighinternational.org (accessed June 1, 2010).

10. Tim Graham and Peter Archer, *William HRH Prince William of Wales* (New York: Atria Books, 2003), 154, 156.

11. University of St. Andrews Web Site, http://www.st-andrews.ac.uk (accessed June 1, 2010).

12. Michelle Tauber, "Frosh Prince: Part Swinger, Part 'Swot,'" *People Weekly*, November 5, 2001, 88.

13. Tim Graham and Peter Archer, *William HRH Prince William of Wales* (New York: Atria Books, 2003), 158.

14. Prince of Wales Web Site, http://www.princeofwales.gov.uk (accessed June 1, 2010).

Chapter 4

PRINCE WILLIAM'S FAMILY

All my hopes are on William now. It's too late for the rest of the family. But William, I think he has it.

—*Princess Diana*

From the time he was born, William has been groomed to be king. His influences obviously include his parents; however, his very fiber is steeped in the history of the monarchy and in his own family. William has been taught his responsibilities almost daily, from the special times he spent with his great-grandmother, the Queen Mother, who died in 2002, to the weekly tea with his grandmother, the Queen; he also learned from his own father, Prince Charles, his mother, the late Princess Diana, and from his brother, Harry. William, now in his late twenties, is described as shy, intelligent, accomplished, and considerate and has his mother's good looks and much of his father's demeanor. Beyond the attributes he inherited, he is also known for his caring attitude, his sense of humor, his intense need to avoid the spotlight, and also his keen knowledge that he will always be within a glaring spotlight. He has lived his life carefully, thoughtfully, and as much as possible, somewhat daringly, all the while knowing he will someday be king. Who he is comes from his ancestry, the history of his country, his parents, and where he has lived, where he has traveled, and where he has been educated.

A VERY SPECIAL RELATIONSHIP: WILLIAM AND THE QUEEN MOTHER

William's great-grandmother was known affectionately to the Royal Family and throughout the kingdom as the "Queen Mum"; to William, she was "Gran-Gran." William and Harry's relationship with Gran-Gran was very special. Although they both had great respect for her, they also liked to spend time with her, joke with her, and tell her about their adventures. She especially loved to hear about William's social life and the latest gossip. Occasionally, William would enjoy tea with her, especially late in her life, and he expressed regret that he was not able to spend time with her when she was younger, like his father had.

The Queen Mum was born a Scottish commoner on August 4, 1900. Throughout her life, she remained one of the most beloved members of the British Royal Family and continued to make public appearances and serve as a patron for about 350 organizations after turning 100 years old. When she was born, Queen Victoria was still the queen, and when she died, her oldest daughter had been the queen for 50 years. She linked the country to its past, was a symbol of the country's history, and was described as a national treasure and a remarkable woman. It was in the late 1930s that her husband, Prince Albert, became King George VI, after his older brother, Edward, abdicated the throne. Then the new King and Queen and their two young daughters were plunged into the very public role of the monarchy at a time when the country was on its way to war with Germany. Throughout the war years, the King and Queen earned the respect and love of their people; while other nations' royalty fled their country for safety, King George and Queen Elizabeth remained in London, visiting bombed areas of the city, encouraging the people to persevere, and comforting those who needed it most. Conveying her optimism to the people of England, Elizabeth wore bright colors instead of black, appeared smiling in newsreels that were sent around the world, and offered uplifting messages in radio speeches.

King George VI and Queen Elizabeth led their country through the war. In 1947, their oldest daughter, Elizabeth, married Philip Mountbatten, and in 1948, the younger Elizabeth gave birth to the Queen's first grandchild, Prince Charles. Also in 1948, the King and Queen celebrated their silver wedding anniversary. In 1952, King George died of lung cancer, and their eldest daughter, Elizabeth, was crowned Queen Elizabeth II; his widow became Queen Elizabeth the Queen Mother.

The Queen Mum died at the age of 101 on March 30, 2002. Her funeral was held at Westminster Abbey. The male members of the Royal Family and, breaking with tradition, the Princess Royal in her naval uniform (the Queen's daughter, known as Princess Anne until receiving her royal title from the Queen) all walked behind her coffin, carried on a gun carriage. Although everyone was deeply saddened by her death, William was especially sad, not only because the two had always enjoyed a special bond, but also because he recognized the difficult and trying times his great-grandmother had been through, and he had felt it easy to unburden himself to her when he felt the need to do so.

ANOTHER SPECIAL RELATIONSHIP: WILLIAM AND QUEEN ELIZABETH II

Throughout history, nannies, governesses, and tutors, not the parents, raised the children of the British aristocracy. Queen Victoria rarely saw her small children for more than an hour a day, after they had been bathed and groomed and were on their very best behavior. Charles did not see his mother very much and rarely had her to himself for any length of time; the schedule was usually an hour at breakfast, a brief meeting at lunchtime, and another half hour at the end of the day before he went to bed. With William's parents, this pattern changed. Charles and Diana were always hands-on parents, and whenever possible, they tried to arrange their busy schedules around William and Harry. Another change was a special relationship that developed between William and his grandmother, or as he called her, Granny, the Queen. She took a special interest in William; after all, the future of the monarchy rested on his shoulders. To be sure, she played an enormous part in William's upbringing and also in his formal training for his role as the future king. A sense of destiny was instilled in William when he was very young. According to Brian Hoey, the author of several books about the Royal Family, the Queen would show William a letter written by Henry VIII or a letter from Queen Victoria to Prime Minister Benjamin Disraeli, "to give him a sense of what his role will be."[1]

The Queen also had a steady hand in William's social life, including whom he would associate with, whom he would date, and certainly whom he might consider marrying and who would thus be queen. To be sure, William could always expect potential girlfriends to come under tough scrutiny, knowing that whoever he wanted to date would have to be of a suitable background. The Queen also had a role in determining where William would go to school, from his early days at nursery school through the university he would attend. She gave William a list of rules that he had to live by when he boarded at Eton and when he went to St. Andrews. Over the years, William found himself going to his grandmother for advice. And although she has never been one to give him a great deal of warmth or affection, there is no doubt she has wanted to indulge him in her own way. She has always been determined to prepare him for his role as King. For William and his Granny, the Queen, the relationship has been unique and quite special.

Since he was born, William has regularly visited Buckingham Palace, Windsor Castle, and the Balmoral and Sandringham estates. And while on these visits as a child, he spent time with his grandmother. Like any proud grandparent and grandchild, the Queen and the young prince played together. When William was a toddler, the Queen was known to crawl around the floor with him. When he was just five, he began taking tea with the Queen every week, a routine that has lasted into William's adulthood. At tea, he would tell her about school, and she would tell him stories about what it is like to be the sovereign queen. After Diana's death, their weekly time together continued and became even more important to William.

These afternoon tea times also often included discussions about riding horses, a favorite pastime of the Queen and other members of the royal families. When William was only five, he won a prize as the third-best young rider at his level and another prize for the best-turned-out rider. While learning horsemanship, he often rode his favorite horse, Trigger. The Queen was quite proud of her grandson's riding skills. In the fall of 1988, after Charles and William completed a riding lesson at

Balmoral Castle, they rode their horses past Queen Elizabeth, who was riding one of her favorite horses, named Greenshield. William called out to her, "Where are you going, Granny? Can I come with you?" The Queen called for him to accompany her on her ride and later, at a picnic lunch, told everyone, "William trotted along so fast on his pony I could barely keep up. I thought the bay would pitch me head first into the road at any minute." An observer of the two riding together noted that few people could lead the Queen on a merry chase; however, William could, he said, adding, "He has inherited his mother's beguiling manner along with the Spencer looks, and like most of the women in his life, his grandmother simply adores him."[2]

A former footman at Windsor Castle who witnessed many of William's visits with his Granny observed that William always seemed eager to learn everything. "He especially wanted to know about the royal boxes that she is always working on—the blue ones from the Foreign Office and the red ones with all the boring paperwork about her schedule." Her Majesty, he added, "spent just as much time listening to him talk about his water polo and his rugby matches. She always managed to look as if she really cared, asking lots of questions, always filled with enthusiasm for what he was doing."[3]

PRINCE CHARLES AND LADY DIANA SPENCER

As Britain's most eligible bachelor, Prince Charles had no shortage of women vying for his heart. The fact that they might someday be queen helped the interest, of course. When Charles was a young man, the women seen with the Prince were a constant topic in the media: Whom would the Prince marry? When would he marry? Marrying and producing an heir was a royal duty, and as heir to the throne, he was certainly cognizant of this. Charles had been encouraged by his great-uncle, Earl Mountbatten, to play the field. In 1974, the latter wrote a letter to Charles, saying, "I believe, in a case like yours, the man should sow his wild oats and have as many affairs as he can before settling down but for a wife he should choose a suitable, attractive and sweet-charactered girl *before* she met anyone she might fall for."[4] Of the women romantically linked to the Prince in the 1970s was Camilla Shand, later known as Camilla Parker Bowles, the daughter of a former cavalry officer. She eventually became one of the most important women in Charles's life. At the time, however, the Royal Family would not condone a marriage to Camilla because of some past circumstances that included several love affairs. Then, in 1973, Camilla married, which ruled her out as a potential royal bride. By late 1980, Charles was convinced that Lady Diana Spencer was the woman he should marry. Diana was the daughter of Earl Spencer, who was at the time the Queen's equerry, an officer of the royal household who attends a member of the Royal Family. When they first met, Diana was 19, and Charles was 31. Their paths inevitably crossed numerous times, and they were often seen together. Diana had been a guest at Buckingham Palace for the Prince's 30th birthday party, and she had also visited Balmoral Castle. Soon the media were enthusiastic about the prospect of Charles and Diana because she appeared to be an ideal princess and suitable to one day be queen. Diana was from a prominent family and was the daughter of an earl. She had no past relationships that would diminish her status or deem her to be unacceptable. She was also young and very attractive. In late 1980, the press began to speculate about an engagement to Diana; however, it seemed that Charles was having difficulty making a decision, despite the intense public scrutiny and extreme pressure on Diana. In February 1981, Charles proposed, and Diana accepted. On July 29, 1981, they were married at St. Paul's Cathedral. The event, carried live on television around the world, was full of glamour and overflowed with the traditional splendor of a fairy tale wedding. Charles wore his dress naval uniform, and Diana's gown, complete with a 25-foot-long train, was made of taffeta and lace. Attending the ceremony were 3,500 guests, and some 600,000 lined the streets of London, hoping to get a glimpse of the couple. It was estimated that approximately 750 million people around the world watched the event.[5] The media portrayed Diana as a shy and beautiful fairy-tale princess, and everyone, it seemed, was looking forward to the fairy tale with the storybook ending. Less than a year after the ceremony, Diana gave birth to a baby boy, Prince William, on June 21, 1982. On September 15, 1984, she gave birth to a second son, Prince Henry, always to be known as Prince Harry.

Although the marriage seemed like a fairy tale from the outside, and although the duty of the prince to produce heirs, specifically sons, was accomplished, it did not take long for problems to develop within the marriage. Some said it was because Charles and Diana had so little in common; others remarked that perhaps they both had emotional needs that could not be satisfied. Diana felt she did not fit in with the Royal Family's way of life, and she disliked the hunting, fishing, and outdoor activities that Charles enjoyed. For his part, Charles found it difficult to cope with Diana and her emotional problems, including a reported eating disorder, and her belief that Charles was having extramarital affairs. It was said he tried to help her but was met with suspicion and was often rebuffed for his attempts. As well, Charles was resentful that Diana was so popular with the public and was becoming so famous around the world. As a result of the marital difficulties, Charles sought solace with his longtime friend and love Camilla Shand Parker Bowles.[6] For much of the 1980s, Charles and Diana went their separate ways, and by the early 1990s, their problems were playing out in the media, in interviews, and in the many books that were written about their relationship. Soon, the marriage's collapse was public knowledge, and in December 1992, the two announced they would separate. Questions about the future included what would happen if Charles became king, whether Charles would remarry, and whether his love affair with Mrs. Parker Bowles, which was public knowledge, would affect his becoming king? In August 1996, the divorce was final. Diana relinquished her title of Her Royal Highness and accepted a financial settlement. She continued to fascinate the world, and the press continued to follow her, capturing her every move, including her romantic liaisons.

PRINCE CHARLES AND LADY DIANA AS THE ROYAL PARENTS OF THE FUTURE KING

A family friend once said, "the most important thing to Diana was to make sure her boys grew up to be normal human beings. And apart from the fact that everyone in the world knows their faces, they are very normal boys. That is Diana's legacy."[7]

From the time William was born, Charles and Diana agreed and disagreed on how William should be raised. Diana's position was "William comes first, always." For Charles, the focus was how to prepare him for the role he would one day play. It was important for him to be well-mannered and cultured and to appreciate and value people from all walks of life. Charles was not concerned with whether William played team sports such as rugby and football, as long as he also excelled at what were to him socially acceptable pastimes such as shooting, hunting, and polo. He said he would like William and his brother too to be brought up "to think of other people, to put themselves in other people's positions. . . . and even if they are not very bright, at least if they have reasonable manners they will get much further in life than by not having them."[8] Diana tried to enable her sons to manage their lives beyond being a member of the Royal Family. She made sure they knew the palace servants and encouraged them to be in the royal kitchen and learn how to prepare their favorite meals. She also took William and Harry out of the palace to visit places such as McDonald's and Burger King occasionally. Although Charles did not approve of forays into the kitchen or to restaurants not befitting the Royals, Diana felt it was important. Perhaps one reason for his disapproval was that Charles had never been anything but a royal, and he had always adhered to the royal rules. Diana did not know all the rules and was not inclined to learn them. She did not want her eldest son to be raised in a household that was stuffy and strict, the kind of atmosphere Charles was very much used to. She took both her boys to hospitals, soup kitchens, and shelters for the homeless. She wanted them to be aware of suffering and unpleasantness and how to manage in the world outside the palace walls. She wanted them to have an understanding of people's emotions, insecurities, and distress and to go to areas where perhaps no one in the Royal Family had ever been before. She gave them tips on how to make small talk and how to work a crowd.

William, unlike the royal children before him, was shown affection in public by his mother. She saw nothing wrong or unusual in this behavior; however, Charles's form of public affection was a pat on his son's head during a polo match. It certainly was not that Charles loved his eldest son any less than Diana did; rather, it was that royalty conventions prohibited public displays of emotion.

When their divorce was final, Charles and Diana continued to be joined by their two sons, and whatever failures they may have had individually and together, they did have remarkable success in their roles as mother and father to both William and Harry. If Charles and Diana had damaged the monarchy, they likely provided the monarchy a tonic or even its salvation through William, who at the time of the divorce was just 14. He was bright and likeable and was continuing to capture the public's attention. At the end of a marriage that had begun with a fairy-tale wedding, William was emerging as a fresh and appealing star, and he was considered to be the monarchy's best hope. He was poised beyond his years, he was intelligent, and he continued to show his affection for both parents. With Charles, William enjoyed hunting, riding, and all outdoors activities; with Diana, his was a role of her protector, confidant, comforter, and soul mate, and they had an openly affectionate relationship. He learned from both his parents, and the resultant combination gave him an advantage as he grew into his role as the future king. However, William has said more than once that he did not truly want to be who he was meant to be. Diana once said of William being king and the oppressive burden of the role, "William is waiting patiently for the monarchy to be abolished. It will make life so much easier for him!"

PRINCE HARRY

William: "When I grow up, I want to be a policeman and look after you, Mummy." Harry: "Oh no, you can't. You've got to be king!"[9]

Prince Harry, the spare heir as he is sometimes called, is the second son of Charles and Diana. He was born on September 15, 1984, and like his brother, he was born in a hospital, the second member of the Royal Family to be born in a hospital. He was christened Prince Henry Charles Albert David by the Archbishop of Canterbury in St. George's Chapel, at Windsor Castle, in December 1984. Like his older brother, Harry went to nursery school at Mrs. Mynor's School, went to the Wetherby School in London, and attended Ludgrove School. And just like William had, Harry attended Eton College and took trips during his gap year to Australia, Argentina, and Africa. Unlike William, who after his gap year went to the University of St. Andrews, Harry's ambitions were of military service, and in May 2005, he entered the Royal Military Academy Sandhurst, where he completed a training course as an officer cadet; he was then commissioned a second lieutenant in the

Household Cavalry. Following the tradition of charity work and volunteerism, Harry cofounded the charity Sentebale (a word that means "forget me not") with Prince Seeiso of Lesotho in memory of both their mothers; the organization supports orphans and vulnerable children in Lesotho. In February 2008, Prince Harry completed two months' service with the British Army in Helmond province, Afghanistan, as a member of the NATO forces. He was promoted to lieutenant in April 2008, and in January 2009, he began a training course to become an Army Air Corps helicopter pilot. Harry is the patron of six organizations and holds two honorary military appointments in the Royal Navy and the Royal Air Force.[10]

William first met Harry the day after he was born. Diana told a nurse that it was important that the first time William saw his brother, she

Prince William, left, and Prince Harry leave
St. George's Chapel in Windsor after the wedding of
their uncle, Prince Edward, and Sophie Rhys-Jones on
June 19, 1999. (AP Photo/Ian Waldie, Pool)

would be holding him in her arms. Charles told William, "Go on, go and see your baby brother." From the moment they met, Harry was William's "favorite toy." Diana said of Harry, "I picked him up and held him every chance I would get. All children should be spoilt that way, although I don't think it's really spoiling your child to lavish love on them."[11] Unlike William, who had very blond hair, Harry's hair was red like Diana's, before she dyed it blond, and like the rest of the Spencer family. Whereas young William was somewhat difficult to manage as a youngster, Harry, initially at least, was nothing like his older brother. He was shy and somewhat withdrawn, whereas William was described as a "tornado," tormenting everyone around him, including his parents, the Queen, and his classmates. Harry often would hide from other children and shunned attention. Over time, this changed. Just as William was learning manners and how to conduct himself as a royal child and had calmed down from his difficult behaviors, Harry began to act up. Both still had a mischievous streak, however, and visitors and family members alike were often made part of the two boys' games played at Highgrove, where they were able to run free on the grounds, instead of being surrounded by bodyguards. One memorable escapade involved the Queen herself at Balmoral. Using a water pistol, the boys had taken to squirting the guards, even when they stood at attention in full uniform. They then turned their aim at the Queen as she returned from a walk with her dogs, the beloved Corgis. They fired before they realized who it was, as her hair was covered by a kerchief; she stood frozen for a moment, took a tissue from her pocket, wiped her face, and kept right on walking, saying rather matter-of-factly, "Good shot."[12] With all their escapades as two young brothers, it was Diana who often led them in fun. She encouraged both boys' natural playfulness and wanted them to grow up in as normal an atmosphere as possible. Charles, though more serious and more aloof than Diana, was also involved in the boys' lives and was a hands-on parent. He was known to play games with them and to be a willing victim in their boys-will-be-boys games. And although both boys were known for their horsemanship, a skill attributed mainly to their father, they were also excellent swimmers, something they learned from their mother.

Even though he had a more easygoing nature than his brother, Harry has always had a reputation as a royal rascal. Growing up, he was more often reprimanded than his brother was and would often first mimic whoever was disciplining him and then rush off laughing. There is no doubt that Harry idolized his older brother from the very beginning, even though, as is the case in many families, the second-born son is often in the shadow of the older son and finds himself constantly compared to the first born. When that first child is the future king, the stakes are higher, and the pressure to live up is intensified. Despite this, the brothers leaned on each other during the difficult times in their parents' marriage, when they fought nearly constantly, and when they separated and subsequently divorced, and they certainly leaned on each other when Diana died and in their lives going forward.

CAMILLA PARKER BOWLES: CHARLES'S LONGTIME LOVE AND WILLIAM'S STEPMOTHER

Charles: "Your great achievement is to love me."
Camilla: "Oh darling, easier than falling off a chair."[13]

In August 1971, just as Charles climbed off his horse after a polo match near Windsor Castle, he met Camilla Shand. He had never seen her before, and although she was not quite like the women that almost constantly swarmed about him, he thought she was beautiful. A few weeks later, at a dinner party given by the daughter of Chile's ambassador, who was one of Charles's longtime friends, he was introduced again to Camilla. They were clearly taken with each other. As it happened, Camilla's great-grandmother, Alice Keppel, had been the mistress of Charles's great-great-grandfather, Edward VII.

Camilla loved the country life and all its pursuits. She was an accomplished horsewoman and loved foxhunting, and throughout her life, she spent much time at her family's estate south of London. After being educated at Queen's Gate, a boarding school in London, she attended finishing schools in Paris and Geneva. She returned to London and received a substantial inheritance from a distant relative; despite the inheritance, she worked as a receptionist at a decorating firm and enjoyed the company of many friends. In 1966, she met a graduate of the military academy, Andrew Parker Bowles, a lieutenant in the Royal Horse Guards. His father was a distant cousin and confidant of the

Queen Mother and was a page at Queen Elizabeth II's coronation. For seven years, Camilla and Andrew dated. During this time, Charles and Camilla met at the dinner party and hit it off immediately, and Camilla became a good friend and someone with whom Charles could share much of his life. She was not, however, someone the palace deemed acceptable to marry Charles. Despite their friendship, Camilla wanted to marry Andrew, and Charles was devastated when he learned that Camilla and Andrew Parker Bowles were engaged.

On July 4, 1973, Camilla and Andrew were married. In December 1974, Camilla gave birth to her first child, Thomas Henry Charles, and Prince Charles was the child's godfather. By this time, he had made strides in forgetting about his love for Camilla and was dating many women, including Lady Jane Wellesley, the daughter of the Duke of Wellington, and Georgina Russell, the daughter of England's ambassador to Spain. He also dated Lady Sarah Spencer, and while visiting her family home in Althorp, England, in 1977, he met Sarah's sister, Diana Spencer, who was 16 at the time and home after a year away at a Swiss finishing school. While he dated other women, and in fact proposed marriage to one of them, he continued to maintain a very special relationship with Camilla. It was Camilla who helped Charles determine his life's focus, which turned out to be bettering society through nonprofit work, rather than military or diplomatic roles. He said Camilla was his sounding board and someone on whom he could always rely. It was Camilla to whom Charles turned when his beloved friend and mentor, Lord Mountbatten, was killed by IRA terrorists.

While he was in mourning, he once again met Diana Spencer in the summer of 1980. At the time, she was 19 and working as a part-time kindergarten teacher in central London. When she expressed her sorrow for his loss, Charles was touched and also captivated by her beauty and shyness. It was soon felt that Diana would make an excellent wife for Charles. She was from one of England's oldest families, she was a virgin, and she was young. Additionally, by now, Charles was 32 years old, and he was being pressured to marry and produce an heir. Diana seemed to be a good choice for marriage and someone acceptable as the future queen. Camilla seemed delighted by the prospect. Charles balked at the idea of proposing marriage, hoping that Camilla would divorce her husband, and they could then be married. He did propose, however, and did so in the gardens at Camilla's home. Once Charles and Diana were engaged, the media constantly pursued Diana. After their wedding, and through the birth of their two sons, all seemed to be well. Unfortunately, it in reality was not, and Charles continued to love and often see Camilla.

Charles moved out of Kensington Palace and into his estate at Highgrove in 1987. In 1988, Diana confronted Camilla at a birthday party for Camilla's sister. After their strained and difficult conversation, Charles took Diana home, chastising her for her behavior. He later called Camilla to apologize. Diana also on several occasions spoke with the Queen about the marriage in hopes that she would intervene. The Queen, listening patiently and calmly, later stated she sometimes felt she had failed her daughter-in-law. Charles and Camilla's relationship continued, and it was not until May 1991 that the public became aware of all the turmoil within the royal marriage. The media noticed that Camilla and Charles were vacationing in Italy without their spouses, and a month later, they were seen together at Highgrove when they received a call that William had been taken to the hospital with a head injury. Whereas Diana refused to leave William's bedside, Charles, after seeing his son, continued on with his schedule. The media wrote extensively about Charles's behavior while his son was injured. After a great deal of media attention, with their life together and their lives apart splashed on the front pages of every newspaper, the two separated, and the marriage eventually ended.

Both William and Harry knew about Camilla Parker Bowles, and when they were old enough to understand such things, they also knew about their father's infidelity and all the rumors surrounding their long love affair. Their mother's famous quote that there were three people in their marriage was well known. And William was often Diana's confidant, despite his age when his parents separated and divorced. No doubt, he heard it all, from both parents, from friends, and from the press, some of which he believed, and some of which he was shielded against. He did not meet Camilla until June 1998 when he was a student at Eton. When the two met, William was just 16; when he entered the room, she nervously curtsied, and William chatted with her, trying to make her feel more at ease. Always taking on the role of peacemaker, he endeavored to make peace here as well and was willing to forgive and forget all that had transpired throughout the years, a task that would seem daunting to many, considering the role Camilla was said to have played in destroying his parents' marriage. What both boys seemed to want now, just a year after their mother's death, was harmony and their father's happiness.

Nearly eight years after Diana's death, Charles, His Royal Highness, the Prince of Wales, was finally able—at long last, it could be said—to marry his longtime love, Camilla Parker Bowles. Upon their marriage on Saturday, April 9, 2005, Camilla became known as Her Royal Highness, the Duchess of Cornwall. They were married first in a civil ceremony at Windsor Guildhall that was attended by 30 friends and family members; a second service of prayer and dedication was held at St. George's Chapel, Windsor Castle, and was attended by 750 well-wishers, including the Queen, who wore a white suit, a matching broad-brimmed hat, black gloves, and an expression that members of the press described as sour, sullen, and cross. The Queen chose not to attend the civil ceremony; the official explanation was that she did not want to overshadow the happy couple, which did not fool anyone.

The Queen was not the only one unsupportive of the marriage. Several of Diana's friends spoke openly about their distaste. A poll in the Sunday London *Times*, conducted the week before the wedding, showed that 73 percent of Britons did not want Camilla to be queen and that 58 percent wanted Prince William, not Charles, to succeed the Queen. The news from London's *Daily Telegraph* was even more damaging. Its poll showed that 69 percent of Britons did not want Charles as their next king and that most believed his marriage to Camilla would weaken the monarchy. Although these opinions mattered to the monarchy, it was England's beloved Queen Mother, one of the most popular members of the Royal Family, and someone who considered Diana to be spoiled and neurotic, and who had forbade her name to be mentioned in her presence, who actively loathed Camilla. Charles and Camilla's marriage reminded the Queen Mum of another time in the monarchy's history, when Edward VIII abdicated the throne and married Wallis Simpson. The Queen Mum remained convinced that all that had transpired during that difficult time had contributed to her beloved husband's death. She had made her daughter, the Queen, promise that she would never allow Charles to marry Camilla, and while the Queen

Mum was alive, this promise was kept. When she died in March 2002, this impediment to the marriage was removed, and Charles, though always close to his grandmother despite her dislike of Camilla, wasted no time in telling his love the news. Events toward Camilla's legitimacy in royal appearances and toward their marriage then moved along quickly, and the two were married in 2005. Whether Camilla will continue to be the Duchess of Cornwall, or the Princess Consort, should Charles ascend to the throne someday, or will be Queen Camilla, is not known; however, it is known that Queen Elizabeth II is not in favor of Camilla ever being queen.[14]

Of course, in attendance at both the ceremonies and at the luncheon at Windsor Castle afterward were William and Harry. By this time, both had gotten to know Camilla and were supportive of their father and his second marriage. Before the couple left the ceremony, William and Harry kissed Camilla on both cheeks and were photographed with her for the first time. They also decorated their father's Bentley and threw confetti as the happy couple left for their honeymoon. Eight years after Diana's death, Charles and Camilla were finally together.

A PRINCESS'S TRAGIC DEATH—PRINCE WILLIAM'S ENDURING TRAGEDY

> He needs to be treated differently because he is different. It's no good Diana pretending he can have a normal life, because he can't.
>
> —*Barbara Barnes, William's first nanny*

Diana may have been the first member of the Royal Family to actually make connections with people from all walks of life and in all sorts of human conditions, from people afflicted with leprosy to people stricken with AIDS and terminal cancer to children born to drug-addicted mothers. She championed causes that included opposition to the proliferation of land mines and aid to battered wives. Her beauty, her charm, and a vulnerability that was combined with mischievousness captivated most everyone. She was the mother of the second and third in line to the British throne and did not care who noticed when she returned home from a trip abroad as she lovingly scooped up her sons and did not want to let them go. She did not care about being royally correct when she publicly showed them affection or shared in their unabashed joy on an amusement ride or sat down at a fast food restaurant with them to share a meal. So on the terrible early morning of her tragic death, it was no wonder the world was shocked and saddened, and many wondered what might happen to her two beloved sons.

When Charles and Diana divorced, the paparazzi continued to follow Diana, and the press continued to report on her romantic liaisons, one of which was with Dodi al-Fayed, the son of the Egyptian owners of the famous London department store Harrods. Diana was with Dodi on the night of August 30, 1997. In the early morning hours of August 31, Diana and Dodi were attempting to escape pursuing photographers, or paparazzi, when their car crashed into a concrete pillar in a Paris tunnel. Both Diana and Dodi died in the crash. Diana's death was an enormous shock, and the world mourned. It was estimated that tens of millions of people watched the funeral service on television. Diana had seemed to be the essence of compassion, duty, style, and beauty, and all over the world she was a symbol of humanity and rights for the poor. In his eulogy at the funeral service held at Westminster Abbey on September 6, 1997, her brother, Earl Spencer, said, "I stand before you today the representative of a family in grief, in a country in mourning, before a world in shock. We are all united not only in our desire to pay our respect to Diana . . . but, rather, in our need to do so."[15]

In addition to the tears shed by the thousands gathered along the funeral route, there were acres and acres of flowers, signs, and messages to the Royal Family. As the cortege carried Diana's body through the streets of London, her two sons, who she once said were her best friends, walked behind the carriage, between their father and their uncle and grandfather. Diana was buried in a private ceremony at the Spencers' ancestral home in Northamptonshire. Her life continues to be celebrated throughout the world, and many are still fascinated by this young woman who was likened to a fairy-tale princess. After Diana's death in May 1997, Charles grew much closer to his sons, and it seemed as if his relationship with them changed, providing for more emotion, more understanding, and a more open relationship than perhaps either William or Charles had ever envisioned. When he heard the news of Diana's death, he reportedly grieved openly and paced the floor alone while wondering how to tell his two sons. William had had a difficult night, his sleep interrupted continually, and when Charles came to his bedroom at Balmoral to tell him the news, he sat on the edge of William's bed, and dispensing with the long British tradition of a stiff upper lip, he and his oldest son held each other and cried. William wondered how they would tell Harry, still asleep in his bedroom just down the hall. Together, they went to Harry, woke him, and told him the news. The three then wept unashamedly, their sobs audible to the staff and aides standing close by.[16]

The Queen, a firm believer in keeping busy and to a routine, encouraged Charles and the boys to maintain appearances and attend church. She instructed the Balmoral Castle switchboard to hold all calls coming in for the boys. She also required that newspapers be temporarily banned and ordered that the television and radio inside the castle be disconnected, all in hopes of shielding William and Harry from further news. Charles told William and Harry about their mother being pursued at high speed by paparazzi at the time of the crash, and this

The Prince of Wales looks toward his sons Prince William, left, and Prince Harry as they wait for the coffin of Princess Diana to be loaded into a hearse after their mother's funeral service in Westminster Abbey on September 6, 1997, in London. (AP Photo/John Gaps III, Pool)

news and the resulting investigations furthered the boys' wariness and suspicion about the paparazzi and media in general. After all, their parents' lives had been splashed across the pages of newspapers for years, and now the press was thought to have a hand in their mother's death. Charles flew to Paris to accompany Diana's casket back to England, and at Balmoral, Tiggy Legge-Bourke, the boys' nanny for years, arrived to be with William and Harry.

The Queen was adamant that no special treatment be given for Diana and certainly opposed a full state funeral, believing they were intended only for kings and queens, even though by order of the monarchy and a vote in Parliament, such a funeral could be extended for others, as was the case for the funeral of Winston Churchill. The day after hearing about their mother's death, William and Harry were told about London being overwhelmed with flowers, left at the palace gates and left at or tied to monuments, lampposts, trash bins, park benches, and tree branches. Over the next days, there were more and more flowers and mourners who refused to leave. Public resentment toward the Royal Family grew; the public wanted to know why the Queen, whose subjects were so clearly in mourning over the "People's Princess," remained at Balmoral. William wondered why as well. He asked Charles, "Why are we here when Mummy is in London?" Polls showed that nearly two out of three Britons believed Diana's death would bring down the monarchy, and there were calls for Charles to step aside in favor of William. As had his mother, William had an ability to know the mood of the people, and Charles turned to his son for advice on what to do about the funeral.

William wanted to know what the telegrams that arrived at the castle said and who had sent them. He wanted to know why the family was staying in Scotland and why his grandmother remained silent. He also insisted that no matter how long the funeral procession route was, he and Harry would march behind their mother's coffin. A palace insider said at the time, "It is touching how William and Prince Harry have pulled together when their world is falling apart. Diana would have been very proud. They are very, very brave." Everyone, it seemed, was struck by William's strength of character and his remarkable courage. After discussion and persuasion by Charles and others, the Queen decided everyone would leave for London. Upon their arrival, she and her husband surveyed the mountains of bouquets, stuffed animals, and notes left in honor of Diana. The Queen then addressed her people and paid tribute to Diana and stated she had admired her and respected her, especially for her devotion to her two boys. William expressed his gratitude to a crowd at Kensington Palace, where Diana and the two boys had lived.[17]

Charles, William, and Harry went to Chapel Royal on the eve of the funeral to privately be with their mother.

> The coffin lid was carefully lifted to reveal Diana, serenely beautiful, the photos of her sons and her father and the rosary from Mother Teresa clasped in her alabaster hands. Tears streamed down William's face at the sight of his mother; Harry, trembling, refused to look . . . after only a few fleeting seconds, the coffin lid was gently closed. William then carefully arranged a spray of white tulips at the head of the coffin, while Harry placed a wreath of white roses he had chosen at the opposite end. Atop the wreath was the square white card on which Harry had simply and boldly written MUMMY.

The next morning, William and Harry waited for their mother's coffin to begin the longest walk of their young lives.[18] Their father, their grandfather Prince Philip, and their uncle Earl Spencer walked with them behind the carriage that carried their mother's coffin. It was estimated that more than 2.5 billion watched the funeral on television, and an estimated 1.5 million mourners lined the route. William and Harry walked stoically past the crowds. "As the boys appeared, everybody who was near them averted their eyes. If you had thought about Diana's sons for six days, to look at them now was impossible. People stared at the road, waiting for the coffin to pass," noted one of the mourners. William looked numb; his eyes, partially shielded by his blond hair, were riveted to the ground.[19]

Ten years after Diana's death, a church service was held to mark the anniversary. As part of marking the event, William and Harry also planned a memorial concert they said would be full of energy, fun, and happiness. Titled "The Concert for Diana," the event was held on July 1, 2007, which would have been Diana's 46th birthday. The star-filled concert, held at London's Wembley Stadium, included a specially prepared tribute composed by Andrew Lloyd Webber and a performance by Diana's good friend Elton John. Elton John had also performed at the funeral service at Westminster Abbey, where he sang the song "Candle in the Wind 1997" ("Goodbye, England's Rose"), which reduced many of the mourners to tears. He did not perform the song again until the 10-year anniversary concert. Within minutes of going on sale, the first 22,000 tickets to the concert sold out. The proceeds, estimated to be more than $10 million, were divided up among Diana's favorite charities. Both William and Harry were determined to make the concert a fund-raising event like no other. Williams said, "First and foremost, the evening is for her—it's all about remembering our mother. It's got to be the best birthday present she ever had."[20]

The beautiful, famous, complicated Diana, one of the most celebrated women in the world, died violently and tragically at the age of only 36. She left behind millions who adored her, respected her, and wondered about her, and she left behind two young sons, which made her death all the more heartbreaking. Diana once said that her two sons were her most splendid achievement, and her influence on both William and Harry was seen from the moments of their birth and continues today. From the beginning, Diana vowed that she would raise her children on her own terms, and she knew it would not be easy. Her decisions were often at odds with Charles, with the palace and the royal advisors, and with the Queen herself. Neither William nor Harry has been particularly shielded from public view, as most children of the Royal Family were in the past. Over the years, the British media for the most part honored requests that the boys be left alone so that they could live their lives as normally as possible, and upon Diana's death, the Royal Family requested the media honor the same request as her two sons came to terms with the tragedy.

All throughout his life, William has favored his mother in his looks. By the time he entered university, he was the mirror image of his mother. He was tall at six feet, two inches, had an athletic build, had the same blond hair, and was soft-spoken; he also had the same downcast blue eyes. And although Charles has had a deep influence on both sons, Diana's continuing influence on their lives and their particular destinies is even more profound, and many of the descriptions of Diana also easily apply to William, such as sensitive, determined, and caring, with a sense of humor and a penchant for fun.

Two months before the fatal car crash that killed Diana, she confided to friends that she hoped William would ultimately handle the media with the same grace and ease as John F. Kennedy Jr. When President Kennedy's son (whose own life would end tragically as well) heard this, he said the situations were not comparable. The pressures on both Diana's sons, he said, were far greater and more relentless than any he had been forced to suffer through. The fact remains that the public cares a great deal about the two young men who walked slowly behind their mother's casket, just as the public cared deeply for the young man who saluted his father's cortege in November 1963. It cannot be denied that Diana lives on in both of her two sons, and her influence on the future king is undeniably eternal.[21] Both William and Harry have grown into fine young men, and Diana deserves much of the credit. P. D. Jephson, Diana's former private secretary and author of *Shadows of a Princess: Diana, Princess of Wales 1987–1996*, said, "The future monarch was King William V, and the Princess took none of her responsibilities more seriously than this—to prepare her children for life in the public eye. She concentrated instead on passing on to William the art of being royal."[22]

NOTES

1. Janice Min, "Prince Dreamboat," *People Weekly*, July 1, 1996, 72+.

2. Joanne Kaufman, "Happy Birthday, Prince Charming," *People Weekly*, June 26, 1989, 30+.

3. Christopher Andersen, *After Diana* (New York: Hyperion, 2007), 41–42.

4. Philip Wilkinson, *The British Monarchy for Dummies* (Chichester, West Sussex, England: Wiley, 2006), 323.

5. Ibid., 324–25.

6. Ibid., 325.

7. Alex Tresniowski, et al., "Boys to Men," *People*, June 4, 2007, 88–94.

8. Brian Hoey, *Prince William* (Phoenix Mill, England: Sutton, 2003), 55.

9. Christopher Andersen, *Diana's Boys* (New York: William Morrow, 2001), 91.

10. Prince of Wales Web Site, "Biography of Prince Harry," http://www.princeofwales.gov.uk/personalprofiles/princewilliamprinceharry/princeharry/biography (accessed June 7, 2010).

11. Christopher Andersen, *Diana's Boys* (New York: William Morrow, 2001), 63–64.

12. Christopher Andersen, *After Diana* (New York: Hyperion, 2007), 64.

13. Ibid., 79.

14. Christopher Andersen, *After Diana* (New York: Hyperion, 2007), 27, 30.

15. Earl Spencer, "The Eulogy," *Newsweek*, September 15, 1997, 24–30.

16. Christopher Andersen, *Diana's Boys* (New York: William Morrow, 2001), 17.

17. Ibid., 22–29.

18. Ibid., 30.

19. Ibid., 31.

20. Christopher Andersen, *After Diana* (New York: Hyperion, 2007), 299.

21. Christopher Andersen, *Diana's Boys* (New York: William Morrow, 2001), 6.

22. Ibid., 143–44.

Chapter 5

THE PRINCE, THE PRESS, SECURITY AND PROTECTION, AND HIS ROYAL DUTIES

Prince William once said to a classmate at Eton, "When you've seen your mother come home in tears because she was being pursued by bloody photographers, you can understand why I hate them so much." When he was older, he said, "I still don't like having to pose for cameras but when I have to do so, I do it . . . just to please my father. I look on it as a duty. That doesn't mean I enjoy it but I understand it's a necessity, a duty."[1]

When William was a boy, the constant media presence was always upsetting. Even though his public appearances were carefully selected and staged, and he was usually with one or both of his parents when the media was present, he was shy and found it difficult to manage the commotion, the aggressiveness, the cameras, and the shouting of questions. Despite awkwardness with the press as a child, when he was close to his mother or father, he often seemed quite natural at appearances and engagements; however, he was very young when he first saw his mother hounded, constantly followed, and nearly hunted down by the press, and it had a negative effect on him. As a result of their being ever present, from an early age he hated the press reporters and photographers. When his mother died in Paris in 1997, the car she was riding in was being chased by the paparazzi, and William was always troubled by the media's role in her death. His anger at the media intensified, and many wondered how he would deal with the press the rest of his life when he felt strongly that the press corps had played a role in his beloved mother's death. To be sure, both Diana and Charles, and then William and Harry too, have been hounded more than other members of the Royal Family; coverage of their lives was nonstop and very hard to avoid. Such aggressiveness by the press toward these Royals has been called unfair, and no one could blame William for his shyness, impatience, and even hatred for at least some of the members of the media.

As a boy, William was purposely shielded from the press. There was a tacit agreement honored by the newspaper editors that he would be left alone until he finished his education. Despite this agreement, there were photo opportunities granted at strategic times. The prince knew how to give the "royal wave" and also knew, as he stood by or walked with a member of the family, whom he could trust, when he should speak, and whose hand he should shake. The palace knew it was important and vital to the monarchy to show the family living as a family and at appropriate royal appearances. Walkabouts with the public were important both to the Royals and to the public. These public appearances and engagements attended by all the Royals were obviously photographed. And although all this was normal and worked efficiently most of the time, there were times when the press was more aggressive and certainly more than bothersome. His parents' marriage and divorce were played out in the press, and each used the press against each other to some degree. William was shielded from all of this while away at school. While at Eton and St. Andrews, students were expressly told they would be disciplined and perhaps expelled if they spoke to the press about their classmate the prince. Many of his classmates were very loyal to William, even protecting him when necessary. However, William quickly found out that he was not able to visit a shop without seeing some new splash, often ugly and sensationalized, about his mother or father. When the family went on vacation, whether it was skiing in Switzerland, visiting a theme park, whitewater rafting on a river in Colorado, or visiting a private island, the press covered the trip, wanting quotes, wanting the story, and reporting to their readers what a royal did or said. Along with a shield against publicity came a prince who was somewhat of an unknown quantity to many of his future subjects. Especially as a teenager, at the arranged photo ops, he appeared shy and somewhat distant. Photographers would complain that they would take rolls of film and not get any of William smiling.

William's wariness of the press was likely inherited from his famous mother and was also the result of being the heir to the throne. He is said to have hated the paparazzi, which could seemingly emerge from nowhere to pursue his mother and anyone with her, including her children. When he was older and had time off from school, he avoided appearing in public with Diana, preferring instead to spend time with his father at the secluded Balmoral estate in Scotland.

Unfortunately, William's cocooned life and an imposed zone of privacy could not go on forever, and the press at one point stopped respecting his privacy. When he was older, he became fair game, as was expected. After Diana's death, there was sensitivity to inflicting more grief on William and Harry. Another agreement was reached between the palace and the press: coverage of both princes would be restricted to authorized photo opportunities. However, many reporters believed that an 18-year-old was fair game, especially one second in line to the throne. Richard Kay, a respected correspondent who covers the Royal Family for London's *Daily Mail* newspaper said, "There are certain things the public has a right to know. We pay an awful lot of money for the upkeep of the family."[2]

When William turned 18 and was considered "of age," he bid farewell to his cosseted boyhood. Although he was able to order a beer in a pub, he also could expect to have more intrusions in his life. However, and without doubt, William remained publicity-averse, and his dislike of the media attention was clear. As part of his momentous birthday, he agreed to release answers to questions submitted by a press representative and allowed a cameraman and a photographer to film him at school and take behind-the-scenes photos of him. The highlights of the press release included information such as the following: William enjoyed action movies, he would rather wear casual clothes, and he enjoyed dancing. He also said he looked forward to taking a year off before starting university and would not take on any royal duties until his graduation. In essence, he was very much like most 18-year-olds.[3]

As his first official public engagement, William, along with Camilla and Charles, appeared at an event held at London's Somerset House that marked the 10th anniversary of the Press Complaints Commission, a government watchdog agency that sets guidelines for the media. It was also a time used to thank the press for keeping a respectful distance from William and Harry since Diana's death and a chance to attempt to persuade more than 500 journalists in attendance to maintain the same respectful distance until Harry turned 18 the next year. William and Charles arrived at the event together and, with drinks in hand, worked the room, talking to reporters and editors. William, at six feet, two inches tall, towered over many of the guests. One observer, *Tatler* magazine editor Geordie Greig, noted that William was "surprisingly at ease" and that he managed to get the phone numbers and e-mail addresses of several single women. One female staffer at the *Daily Telegraph* noted, "Prince William was not at all shy about asking. He was very confident. I must say he possessed a great deal of poise for a nineteen-year-old." The event served as an opportunity for William and Charles to win over the press and hopefully keep them at a distance as much as possible.[4]

When William spent time with the Queen, especially during their afternoon teas, he learned how important it was to keep his emotions to himself and maintain stoicism. Many wondered whether William was able to keep his feelings in check or was suppressing them, especially in light of his mother's death and given that both his parents' relationships had played out in the press, and individuals closest to his parents were writing books and giving interviews and telling stories, whether true or untrue. William was blocking all the unpleasantness out, rather than facing it, as much as possible. Many close to him noted that he was sinking in a discernibly darker mood, whereas Harry, always more outgoing than William, was able to let out his feelings and was quick to share them with others and then move on. In a rare display of temper as he was returning from a foxhunting expedition, William yelled obscenities at a photographer and then forced him into a ditch. The photographer, Clive Postlethwaite, was waiting for the hunting party when Charles rode by first, and then William saw him and lost his temper. As William rode his horse toward the cameraman, the latter dropped his camera and jumped into a ditch to avoid being trampled by the horse.[5] The incident was one more example of William's difficulty dealing with the continued media presence.

The press, the media, the paparazzi—whatever term they are known by—will always be a part of the life of a royal. And although most royals understand this, and though William has had to learn to manage the media and live his life in the midst of reporters' and photographers' presence, the media does understand what it means to deal with the palace and any potential backlash. The media remained aware of the sympathies toward both William and Harry as they grew up, and both William and Harry, as men, now understand they cannot and will not be shielded any longer. The press was completely absolved of having any part in Diana's death, yet William maintains his intense dislike of the press; he has learned how to use it when he needs to and has come to understand that from his recent engagement to his upcoming marriage to his ascension to the throne, if and when that occurs, the media will always be a part of his life.

Just as Diana and Charles learned that sometimes photo opportunities are required and are worthwhile, there are times when privacy and respect are also expected. From an early age, William hated having his picture taken. On one occasion, Diana told William, when he put his hands in front of his face to avoid the cameras, "Take your hands away Wills, you'll have to get used to this. It's never going to go away."[6] Diana taught both her sons to accept the inevitable burdens of being a member of the Royal Family. One of her bodyguards, Ken Wharfe, said that Diana lectured young William when he cowered from photographers: "She dealt with the media incredibly well and taught Will and Harry that it's part of their life too. She said [to William], 'You better get used to it. Just smile and wave and move on.'" At the same time, she made sure the boys got out and met people and enjoyed and experienced life. She dressed them in jeans and took them to movies and amusement parks, and when the press followed, she kept them going and taught them it was part of their lives.[7]

THE PRINCE'S SECURITY AND PROTECTION

Throughout history, the Royal Family has always lived within a bubble of tight security. The first Queen Elizabeth certainly had to be careful;

from employing tasters of her food to being escorted while walking about the royal grounds, she was wary of everyone and everything. For the current Queen Elizabeth, although she may not have someone taste her food before she takes a bite, the ring of security that surrounds her is likely even tighter than for her ancestor. William has always had a security detail surrounding him. During his rides in his pram with his nanny around the gardens of Kensington Palace, protection officers walked along. When he went to nursery school, the building was swept by the police for listening and other potentially disastrous devices; the teachers and staff were interviewed. As his educational settings changed, so did the details of his protection. At Eton and at St. Andrews, William lived with his security detail nearby, in the room next door and camped out at building entrances; and whenever he went shopping, strolled through the campus grounds, visited friends, or went for a beer, so did his protection officers. He was always cautioned not to evade his detail, and he understood why they were always about, like it or not. At Eton, where the country's elite come to study, classmates may have noticed the royal in their midst only by the uniformed policemen standing nearby; the plainclothes bodyguards were a bit more difficult to spot but were always present as well. Additional security cameras were installed, and the local police forces were on alert at all times. And although great pains were taken to treat William like any other student, or like any other guy when he was out and about, there was no mistaking that William, the future king, was there. When he practiced driving and earned his driver's license, he did so with a security officer in the car seat next to him. Life with a policeman at his side at all times must seem cumbersome and tiresome at times, but it is necessary, and William understands it and accepts it.

The Royal Family was on its annual summer vacation at Balmoral in Scotland in 2001 when the Queen was called about two planes slamming into the World Trade Center and the Pentagon. Throughout the day and into the night, the Queen and the princes Philip, Charles, William, and Harry were glued to the images carried live by the BBC. One member of the household staff recalled the Queen being very emotional: "She does not let her feelings show very often, and when she does it is very moving." The following day, the Queen noted that she was "watching developments in growing disbelief."[8] William and Harry had visited the United States with their mother in 1993, and both had developed a great interest in all things American.

After the attacks, William wanted to show his solidarity with the American people; even though the government's Foreign Office released official statements with the Queen's signature, William wanted something more clear and heartfelt. He suggested a musical tribute at Buckingham Palace. During the Changing of the Guard ceremony two days later, the Coldstream Guards band opened with a rendition of "The Stars and Stripes Forever" and then played the "Star-Spangled Banner" before ending with "When Johnny Comes Marching Home." The hundreds of tourists outside the palace gates, many of whom were stranded in England after the attacks, burst into applause and cheered. The next day, during a memorial service at St. Paul's Cathedral held in honor of those who had perished in the attacks, the Queen stood to sing "The Star-Spangled Banner," marking the first time any British monarch had sung the American anthem. Richard Kay, a columnist for London's *Daily Mail,* noted, "The Queen does not 'sing' national anthems. Her mouth never opens when they are played. It was the ultimate sign of unity, friendship, and support for America."[9] The attacks prompted heightened security for all the Royals, who were deemed to be potential terrorist targets. After the 9/11 attacks, when Great Britain joined with the United States in the war on terrorism, William and Harry's security detail was tightened. As a university student living in a private residence, William was considered as potentially the most vulnerable member of the Royal Family, and additional teams of armed bodyguards were added to his protection team.

Even before 9/11, Charles was said to be fearful of William's vulnerability at St. Andrews, and deliberate steps to protect the future heir were taken. Although first-year students generally live in shared rooms, William, as a first-year student, was assigned to live at St. Salvator's College, or Sally's, as it is known, in a single room. A new electronic lock was installed on the front door, and his personal bodyguard was assigned to the room next door. On the Monday after moving in to his room, as William made his way from his residence hall to the History of Art department, he caught sight of a television crew. All media had been asked to leave the university on Sunday, and William was surprised by the clear breach of the agreement that had been struck between the palace and the press. Two days later, as he walked to his first lecture, his protection officer told him that a film crew was in town. This was reported to the university, and the presence of the crew was investigated and reported to Prince Charles. After the film crew refused to identify themselves, a heated exchange ensued, and they finally admitted they were a freelance crew working on a documentary commissioned by William's uncle, Prince Edward, and his production company, Ardent. Prince Charles was at first disappointed and then enraged. Stating they had permission from the university to film students in restaurants, pubs, shops, and the student union offices, they adamantly denied they had tried to film the prince. Although Charles was indeed enraged by the film crew's presence and the breach of the agreement, William was also furious and spoke with his father several times about the incident. He did not want his presence or his name used in this manner, in a documentary or in a news story about him as a university student. Hearing about the incident, one of Diana's friends noted, "There is a lot of Spencer in William and a lot of his mother. And, like the Princess, if he finds out he is being used he will dump that person and go mad. If Diana thought she was being used she'd go off like a rocket. He is the same."[10]

Unfortunately, this incident was difficult for William and for his fellow classmates, and it caused difficulties between Charles and his brother Edward, who apologized for the intrusion and tried to assure both his brother and his nephew that the film crew was not filming William in particular. The Queen, for whom arguments within the family are a disgrace, tried to remain partial; however, she eventually wholeheartedly backed Prince Charles's decision to go to all lengths possible to protect William and his son's privacy. For its part, Ardent, the documentary film company, had to agree not to make any more royal programs. William was said to feel "let down" by his uncle. One of his prime reasons for selecting St. Andrews, a university in a remote town on the far coast of Scotland, was that it offered him the possibility of escaping the attention of the media. To discover that a member of his own family, someone on whom he had depended and who should understand the need for privacy and personal safety, had allowed the media to be in such close proximity was a great disappointment to the young prince.[11]

Britain's Prince William, left, accompanied by his father, Prince Charles, arrives at the University of St. Andrews in St. Andrews, Scotland, September 23, 2001, where he would take an art history course. (AP Photo/Adam Butler)

Along with the disappointment at being filmed by a company associated with a family member, William was disappointed yet again when it came to his own privacy. When he initially enrolled at St. Andrews, MI5, the United Kingdom's counterintelligence and security agency, performed an electronic sweep of William's room and discovered listening devices that had been planted by the Royal Protection Service as a means of keeping tabs on the student prince, with the approval of Prince Charles. When William confronted his father, demanding to know how he could have permitted such a violation of his privacy, Charles decided his son was right and ordered that William's rooms be swept clean of all eavesdropping devices. However, although the devices planted by the Royal Protection Service were removed, MI5 planted its own devices. Glynn Jones, one of the British military surveillance experts in charge of watching over Diana, stated that every member of the Royal Family is watched around the clock. "Their personal conversations, both on the phone and sometimes person to person, are monitored and recorded and many of their movements are captured on videotape. It's impossible for them to keep any secrets. The most personal things are recorded. Charles, Camilla, and William are always under surveillance by secret service personnel."[12]

For William, living with meticulous security measures, and as a result of such measures, having his friends and his classmates also living amid such strict measures, surely was not easy. William tried to take a defensive approach to life at university and said he would spot those who would try to take advantage him quickly. He declared his intention of living as ordinarily as possible, and initially at least, he preferred to keep to himself, associating with only a few chosen friends, most of them also from Eton and who called him "Wales." He found solace in the library or alone in his room while his classmates were out enjoying life as first-year university students. After joining the polo team, and to keep fit physically, he joined a private fitness club rather than use the campus gymnasium. At first, William wanted space and kept himself away from others as much as possible, and as a result, during his first year, he became a bystander to what his classmates were enjoying. He rarely stayed on campus during the weekends, preferring to drive to Edinburgh to attend parties with friends. And after his first year, he discussed transferring to another school with his father. He said he was bored and lonely. Charles, who listened and counseled, stated that changing would present vast security issues, and that because St. Andrews was William's first choice, he should stand by his decision, adding that homesickness was something that often plagued students. In his second year, William felt more comfortable and moved into an apartment, or flat is it is known in England, in a converted Victorian house. His roommates were a friend from Eton and Kate Middleton, his future on-and-off-again girlfriend. William came to appreciate what St. Andrews offered him as a university student.

William Arthur Philip Louis Wales, or Wills, or William, would never be just one of the guys. But he does try, and for many, that is what matters. All that he inherited from his mother, including his shy grin and his blue downcast eyes and his determination to shrug off some of the restraints that tradition and his pedigree impose on him and on everyone that surrounds him, just may be what keeps the monarchy from becoming obsolete at a time when most of the monarchy's subjects think it needs to modernize. In fact, there are many in the realm who believe that when it is William's time to ascend to the throne, the monarchy will not exist. It was just one of Diana's goals that her children be real human beings and not have a "robotic" childhood like their father had. She herself wanted to be relevant, and she wanted her two sons to be relevant too.[13] Still, both William and Harry are second and third in line to the throne, and keeping them safe is paramount and especially difficult and important in these days of actual and potential terrorism.

THE PRINCE'S ROYAL DUTIES

> William once said, "It's not a question of wanting to be King. It's something I was born into and it's my duty."[14]

As a young boy, William enjoyed somewhat carefree days. His mother was adamant that he have as normal an upbringing as possible and tried to provide days of fun and time with other children as much as possible. As he grew older, however, these days and his innocence too were left behind. It was made clear to him early on that although he needed to fit in and understand ordinary people, royalty was in his blood. From where he would go to school to what functions he would attend to whom he would marry, everything was carefully planned with an eye toward his future as the sovereign king.

From an early age, William had a predetermined role, and his formal responsibilities were gradually introduced. William learned quickly that duty was paramount, and his obligations and responsibilities were instilled in him by his parents and by the Royal Family throughout his early life; it is clear he has had to absorb more than 1,000 years of claims of duty, tradition, and discretion. For the monarchy, duty comes before personal happiness and before any emotions. William understands this and recognizes what his parents and the Queen have given up in the name of duty and country. He also understands the demands that will be made of him in his future; however, he does possess a rebellion that sometimes, although not often, comes out and makes him question the need for such sacrifices in the world where he lives. He compares his life to the lives of royal members of other monarchies and wonders why he is required to do, say, appear, or act as he must. Despite his nature, and his life thus far, it is clear William takes his duties and responsibilities very seriously; his training, since the day he was born, is evident when he takes part in his royal duties.

However, although William is his father's son, with his father's seriousness, obedience, and very life as a royal with all its sacrifice and advantages, he is also his mother's son, with her looks and disposition, her playfulness, her sense of humor, her need of privacy, and who she was as a result of her upbringing as a commoner, with a unique set of a commoner's sensibilities and expectations. Diana gave the monarchy an extraordinary gift when she fulfilled her own duty by producing a male offspring who would someday be king. She gave her and Charles's progeny to the family Windsor and all of England and then raised him with a commoner's hands-on warmth and informality. Diana's influences are often on display. At his first solo foray with the press, one not conducted at St. James's Palace, but rather at a pub where he wore jeans and a red sweatshirt and donned a charming smile, William was relaxed and confident. After a 90-minute chat with the invited tabloid reporters, who were all particularly smitten with the young prince, the reporters had learned absolutely nothing. William had learned from his mother's experiences very well; although he is very much his father's son and has been influenced by his grandmother the Queen, he is also a prince after his mother's heart, and her legacy in particular, is in good hands.[15]

While William was a student at the Ludgrove School, he began to make appearances as a member of the Royal Family, although his parents had long before agreed that he would not undertake any royal engagements alone until he finished his education. He did, however, from an early age, accompany one or both parents on various visits while they were engaged in their royal responsibilities. The thought was that he would learn how to behave and how to perform as a royal by being with his parents and other members of the Royal Family. It was a given, no matter how reluctant William may have been, that he would always have to be on guard, act in a specific way, and appear as a royal. After all, it was his destiny. Even as a boy, he somehow knew this, despite his early escapades of high-spiritedness. William's role, until he finished his education, was always one of appearing with his parents or members of the Royal Family, and almost never one he himself pursued. And even though there was not any sort of on-the-job training for any royal, and he was expected to learn from his parents and other royals, Diana was famous for how capable and hands-on she was at coaching William on his responsibilities, on how to shake hands, how to speak, how to treat others, how to be gracious, and how to act appropriately as a member of the Royal Family.

When William appeared with his famous and beautiful mother, he was, like her, treated not only as a royal but also much like a rock star. His boyishness, his likeness to his mother, and his shyness were quite endearing in his younger years. As a teen and into his adulthood, with his good looks and obvious intelligence, he was nearly always appreciated and celebrated. As a boy, he was often overwhelmed with flowers and cheers from the crowds that always seemed to gather when he was nearby. As a teen, there was often near mass hysteria from the rope lines of young girls that who to see the shy, handsome teen prince. Now that he is an adult, tall and lean, nearly five inches taller than his father, with a shy smile and startling blue eyes, the crowds still gather, and the women still nearly swoon; he is nearly always met with affection and cheers and is still, as he has always been, one of the most popular of royals. For nearly all his life, William has been met with "Willsmania," with near-frantic scenes of girls screaming his name over and over again, throwing flowers at him, and climbing over each other and the barriers in order to get an opportunity to touch him or shake his hand. Along with the throngs of admirers have always been the ever-present members of the media, some respectful, others more aggressive. He has always been shy in the front of the camera, although as he has matured and gained self-confidence and a greater sense of his place and his personal destiny, he has been more able to manage the press and the paparazzi. To be sure, William has always naturally possessed the required sense of duty that is inherent to a member of the Royal Family and, in his case, a future monarch. He has also had the needed charisma his whole life and, thanks to his mother, a star quality that few royals have possessed. These attributes have always served him well and will be required of him well into the future.

Although William had made public appearances with either or both of his parents throughout his young life, his first public engagements began when he was eight. The first was at London's St. Paul's Cathedral in October 1990, for a service to commemorate the 50th anniversary of the London Blitz, the bombing of Britain during the early years of World War II. The next came in May 1991, when he went with his parents to Cardiff, Wales, to attend a service at Llandaff Cathedral on St. David's Day. This public engagement was especially appropriate for William because he was introduced to the principality of Wales, from which he takes his title, the Prince of Wales. On this visit, William attended the church service and met dignitaries and a group of young people dressed in carnival costumes, which amused the eight-year-old prince. While Diana visited members of the military at a Royal Air Force station, William visited an aircraft museum where he sat in a wartime Spitfire airplane and in a Harrier Jet. After such a grand time in a museum that he had all to himself, it was hard for him to leave and join his parents again on their tour. After the success of the trip to Cardiff, Diana decided she wanted both William and Harry to see more of Wales, so she arranged another trip later that same year. Diana took the boys on an ordinary scheduled train from London, and not a special car just for them, and even though there were press on the train, and more photographers and reporters met them at the station in Cardiff, Diana felt that a trip she and the two boys made on their own, and which was not for an official royal engagement, was a good photo opportunity. She had specifically requested that there be no official meetings or formal engagements. Instead, she and the two boys dined at the home of the Queen's representative, Captain Norman Lloyd-Edwards, and attended a rugby match at Cardiff's Millennium Stadium, where they joined in the community singing of the Welsh national anthem. William and Harry have continued to visit Wales throughout their lives on official visits as well as for more rugby games and to meet team players. Over the years, Captain Lloyd-Edwards of Wales got to know William and said of him, "He wasn't like any other boy. Even as a youngster there was a calmness about him that made him stand apart from everyone else . . . it was bred into him, a natural dignity that is . . . unusual in a teenager. . . . he has always shown an enormous sense of responsibility."[16]

Throughout history, members of the Royal Family have been asked to be godparents. For William, the first request came when he was at Eton and just 16 years old. One of William's own godfathers, King Constantine of the Hellenes, a resident of London, asked William to be the godfather to one of his grandsons, Konstantine Alexios, the second child of Crown Prince and Crown Princess Pavlos. William was the youngest of eight godparents and the closest in age to his godson. Prince Charles was the godfather to the couple's first child, a daughter, Maria-Olympia.

When William was in his final year at St. Andrews, he gave an interview to the British Press Association and posed for pictures in exchange for the reporters leaving him alone while at school. In the interview he made it clear that he was not going to take on the many duties required of the Royals after he graduated. "It's not that I never want to. It's just that I'm reluctant at such a young age to throw myself into the deep end." He insisted that the prospect of someday being king did not keep him awake at night, adding that life was just too short to worry about it all.[17]

William has been trained to be the future king from the day he was born. Everything he has done since that momentous day in 1982 has been carefully orchestrated, and whether he wants to be king or not, he has no choice in the matter. Since his graduation from St. Andrews, and throughout his military career since then, the Queen has worked to direct a seamless transition of the monarchy to the next generation, and William has become more active in the decision-making process. The Queen has turned over more of the duties and responsibilities to Charles, who in turn has given William more duties and responsibilities as the next in the line. Those closest to the Queen have stated that she has no intention of stepping down and regards herself as the true head of the Royal Family. She will likely never retire and regards her job as a job for life. She is aware of the polls that signify Charles as somewhat an unpopular candidate for king and of the public's affection for her and for her grandson William. To the monarchy and to the public, William is handsome, dynamic, and charismatic and represents the modern world. He upholds the tradition of the monarchy, yet he connects with the people of the realm and the world in a way no other member of the monarchy is able to.

NOTES

1. Brian Hoey, *Prince William* (Phoenix Mill, England: Sutton, 2003), 158.

2. "Prince Charming," *Newsweek*, June 25, 2000, 44.

3. "The Rising Son: Diana and Charles's Oldest Boy Emerges from Childhood," *People Weekly*, July 3, 2000, 56+.

4. Christopher Andersen, *After Diana* (New York: Hyperion, 2007), 122–23.

5. Ibid., 173.

6. Brian Hoey, *Prince William* (Phoenix Mill, England: Sutton, 2003), 72.

7. Alex Tresniowki et al., "Boys to Men," *People*, June 4, 2007, 88–94.

8. Christopher Andersen, *After Diana* (New York: Hyperion, 2007), 143.

9. Christopher Andersen, *After Diana* (New York: Hyperion, 2007), 142–44.

10. Ingrid Seward, *William and Harry* (New York: Arcade, 2003), 272–73.

11. Ibid., 277–79.

12. Christopher Andersen, *After Diana* (New York: Hyperion, 2007), 174–75.

13. Jumana Farouky, "Like Mother, Like Sons," *Time International* (Europe Edition) 170, no. 8 (2007): 22.

14. Andersen, *After Diana*, 275.

15. Tina Brown, *The Diana Chronicles* (New York: Doubleday, 2007), 481–82.

16. Brian Hoey, *Prince William* (Phoenix Mill, England: Sutton, 2003), 69–70.

17. Christopher Andersen, *After Diana* (New York: Hyperion, 2007), 220.

Chapter 6

A SPORTING PRINCE

When William was just nine months old, he accompanied his parents on a trip to Australia. As Charles and Diana toured the continent, William and his nanny stayed at a sheep station known as Woomargama in the outback of New South Wales. For a break from their travels and all the events and functions that were a part of their trip, Charles and Diana visited William, both to see him and to relax before setting out again to attend dinners and openings and visit dignitaries. Although William was sheltered from all the crowds and reporters and photographers that followed his parents on their trip, the public developed a great fascination with the little prince that was staying in New South Wales; wherever Charles and Diana went, they were asked about how William was doing, what toys he was playing with, and when would they see him. By this time, William was crawling and was quite active; he was described by his beaming parents as "a mini tornado." It was not long before photographers descended on the house where William and his nanny were staying, hoping to catch a glimpse of them taking their afternoon walks on the secluded grounds. It was on this trip that William provided his first photo op for the gathered reporters and photographers. At 9:00

in the morning, with journalists, photographers, and television crews present, William, dressed in a romper suit, performed the crawl that his father had been talking about so much. Although the media had been warned that the little prince might not perform on cue, Charles proudly observed that his son performed like a true professional in front of the cameras and "did everything that could be expected of him." Later that day, Charles presented William with a miniature polo stick to play with. Charles noted, "I suspect the first thing he will do with it is to chew it, the second thing will be to hit me sharply on the nose, but I hope in twenty years' time he will be galloping up this field with me in a bathchair on the sideline." Twenty years later, William would indeed be playing polo, with his father by his side, but with a bath chair nowhere in sight.[1] The polo stick was likely the first piece of sporting equipment William received; however, there were many more to come.

The Royal Family is and always has been very competitive. They also take great pride in a member's success on the field of play, including in William's case. Receiving his first polo stick from his father before he was a year old was more than a hint of what was in store for Prince William. There were many days ahead of swimming, horse riding, polo, football (soccer), hunting, shooting, motorcycle riding, driving go-karts, and golf. When he was not playing and competing, he was watching sports. From an early age, he attended tennis matches at Wimbledon and watched horse racing at the many venues around England. William has always loved participating in and watching sports and has always enjoyed speed, whether in cars and go-karts or on a horse. From his first polo stick at nine months old, William has always been a sporting prince.

When in London, William lived at Kensington Palace. As a child, he went for walks and played in the palace lush gardens, often with Diana or Charles, and more often with his nanny. But though Kensington Palace was his family home, the place that he truly enjoyed as a boy, a place he likely called home, a place where he could behave more like an ordinary boy, was Highgrove House, a large home with vast grounds located in the quiet Cotswold countryside, near Tetbury, Gloucestershire. Highgrove House is currently the family home of Charles, Camilla, William, and Harry and is a home William will someday inherit when Charles becomes king. Highgrove House remains a place both William and Harry still visit and enjoy, especially when they want to get away from it all and relax. When Charles purchased Highgrove in 1980, he transformed the grounds from a working farm into lush gardens and meadows and added such livestock as chickens, sheep and horses, dogs, guinea pigs, and rabbits.

As a young boy at Highgrove, William had many toys, including a replica of a Jaguar automobile that he drove around the grounds at 15 miles per hour. He and Harry had rabbits and guinea pigs to care for, dogs to play with, a tree house to play in, and bales of hay to climb around on. At Highgrove, William also had horses to ride every day. From an early age, William was taught to ride; as a toddler, he spent time just sitting on the horse, and then as a young boy, he was taken out every morning by a groom on his own Shetland pony, which was taken to Balmoral Castle, so that he could continue to ride and take riding lessons there on his own horse. Like his mother, who did not particularly enjoy riding, William was at first somewhat fearful and had to be cajoled into the saddle. He did overcome this initial fear and became an accomplished rider and has continued to ride throughout his life, for pleasure, for hunting, and on the polo field.

PARTICIPATING IN SPORTS AT SCHOOL

Unlike members of the Royal Family before him, William attended nursery and primary schools outside of the palace. At these schools, William took part in all the various programs offered, including music, art, and sports. As well, Charles and Diana firmly believed in being a part of William's education as much as their busy schedules would allow and visited the schools for many of the events and programs. The annual sports day event at the Wetherby School became a regular event on the royal calendar. At the event in June 1987, Diana kicked off her high-heeled shoes and ran barefoot in the mothers' race, winning by three yards. She persuaded Charles to loosen his tie, remove his suit jacket, and take part in the fathers' race. Unfortunately, Charles and William came in last in their race. The next year, Diana won again as William chanted, "My mummy's won, my mummy's won!" He had won his own prize by coming in third in the egg and spoon race. Through 1991, Diana and Charles continued to participate with William in the sports day events at his school, thereby setting an example, both in enjoying sport competitions and in providing her two boys with as much a normal life as possible. Princess Diana was likely the first member of the Royal Family to do something such as kick off her shoes and run barefoot in a race with her son at a school event.

For five years, William also attended Ludgrove School, a preparatory boarding school in Berkshire, England, where he was involved in individual and team sports. While at Ludgrove, he was the rugby and hockey team captain, was a part of the swim team where he was an accomplished swimmer, played on the football and basketball team, participated in clay pigeon shooting, and also represented the school at cross-country running.

SHOOTING, HUNTING, AND FISHING— ROYAL FAMILY SPORTS

Another sport that is inherent to a royal's life, including William's, is that of the shoot. His mother, however, always hated anything to do with guns, and she tried, unsuccessfully, to persuade both William and Harry to not take part in the sport. Despite knowing her strong feelings, William continued to enjoy the sport long into adulthood. He was just four years old when he accompanied Charles on a shoot at Sandringham House, the Royal Family's private Norfolk home for four generations of sovereigns since 1862. Seeing him armed with a toy silver pistol, animal rights activists took great exception to William's presence at the shoot. But despite the continued passionate feelings of animal rights activists, the hunt and the "riding to the hounds" events are something that royals have enjoyed throughout history and consider a right and a tradition. William has enjoyed shooting and hunting since he was a boy, despite his mother's continued hatred of both. Although he had only a toy pistol at his first hunt, William has been attending hunting and shooting events at Sandringham House, at the Balmoral estate, and at other family estates since he turned 16. At one event, a red-capped William was photographed by the press on horseback, sailing over fences in hard pursuit, along with other members of a hunting club, near Highgrove. Animal rights activists were horrified at the prince's taking part in what they deemed to be extraordinarily cruel; defenders of the hunt viewed the sport as just one more cherished British tradition under attack. For his part, William publicly vowed to continue fox hunting. He was denounced on the floor of the House of Commons for his "insensitivity" and "upper-class arrogance."[2] In England, riding to the hounds and fox hunting were outlawed in 2005.

For many in England, and certainly for most of the Royals throughout history, hunting is not only a tradition and a passion; it is also considered exhilarating and entertaining. As William and Harry grew older, they both came to like nothing better than tramping across the fields and moors and through the glens and streams after deer, pheasant, partridges, pigeons, fox, and salmon. When William was just 12 years old, he was allowed to go with his father and grandfather on a "stalking" trip. He had been given lessons on handling a "light 28-bore shotgun," so he was not nervous about handling such a firearm. For years, he had already watched others in the sport, and he knew how the dogs worked in retrieving the birds once they fell to the ground.

Although the Royals no longer fox hunt, most continue to enthusiastically take part in the sport of hunting game and shooting. William continues to be an excellent and enthusiastic horseman and is considered to be natural horseman who shows no fear when riding. He is also considered a skilled marksman, and as a reward for his skill, he was given a .243 rifle crafted by the Scottish gunsmith Michael Lingard in 2003. With a Turkish walnut stock and gold inlay, it cost £20,000. Charles offered to have it engraved with William's coat of arms, but William, a bit less ostentatious than his father, settled for a simple "W."[3] Whereas William is considered an accomplished shot, his father is considered an excellent shot, something that gives William enormous pride. He has always taken great pleasure in his father's success with a gun.

Another sport William continues to enjoy is fishing. For many years, William and his father have been fly-fishing together along the River Dee in Scotland, and when she was able to, William's great-grandmother, Queen Elizabeth the Queen Mother, would accompany them; she had a great love of the sport and delighted in William taking such an interest in it. William once said of the fly-fishing that one of the great attractions is the solitude: "Apart from the sport, I find it is also a great time for thinking."[4]

PLAYING POLO ON HIS FAVORITE HORSES

Just as William takes great pride in his father's abilities with a gun, he is also very proud of his father's accomplishments on the polo field, and William has emulated his father's passion for the sport since first receiving his polo stick as a toddler. The game has always been and continues to be an important part of William's sporting life, and he plays as often as possible.

During his last term at Eton, over a glass of lager at a local pub popular with Eton students for generations, the conversation turned to what he and his friends would do next. At 18 years old, most students were eager to take the next steps, some to the military, some to university, and still others toward travel, trekking about in foreign lands, something not open for a future king. As the future sovereign, William was not quite as eager to leave Eton. He had had five both positive and difficult years at Eton; however, for the most part it had been a good experience because here he could be a student without the media attention that would soon follow him everywhere. What he wanted to do, he told his friends at the pub, was to play polo. To him, it was the perfect life and an excellent way to spend a "gap year," that 12-month sabbatical between secondary school and university studies. As an enthusiastic and skilled player, he thought that moving to Argentina, a country that produced the best players and the best ponies for the game, was an excellent idea. It would be the best way, he was sure, to realize his aspiration of becoming a high-goal player, and importantly for the young prince, it was a long way from his destiny and royal duties. The idea was quickly dismissed by Charles, who noted that the days when princes could behave like playboys and be applauded for it was long gone. And, Charles said, William had to use his time positively and acquire practical experience in helping others less fortunate. Although William could well be headstrong, he could not go against his father's wishes.[5] When William entered St. Andrews, he offered to pay the university fees himself; however, Charles agreed to pay them, but William, he said, would have to pay the expenses associated with his love of polo.

Polo is a game often associated with the rich and famous, and it also represents a glamorous social scene. An avid player, William is always the center of attention, and devotees of the sport focus on his athletic prowess on a horse, his skill in playing the game, his good looks and royal status, and the fact that very often, polo matches are an opportunity to raise money for charities that William supports. It was in 1999 that William and Harry played on the same team as their father for the first time, a special time for both boys, who continue to be proud of their father's abilities on the polo field.

William first sat on a horse and had riding lessons from a groom when he could barely walk. He rides his favorite horses to play polo with an aggressive ability and an enthusiasm shared by his father, brother, and grandfather. And like all of his family, he is a true competitor and likes to win, not just compete. When he began playing the sport, Charles employed one of the world's best, well-known Argentinean instructors to teach William how to play and how to win. Like others on the polo field, William's courage has never been in doubt. Like others, he has had his share of falls, but he has always enjoyed the game, and the more physical it is, the better he seems to like it.

William continues to enjoy the sport of polo and plays regularly to raise money for charities, including the Tusk Trust, an organization formed in 1990 that works to protect wildlife, particularly endangered species; to alleviate alleviates poverty; and to provide financial and logistical support for projects in 17 African countries. William is a royal patron of the Tusk Trust.[6] He also plays in matches to raise money for Centrepoint, a national charity in England that supports homeless young people. As a royal patron of the organization, William, along with his team Cirencester Park Polo Club, played in a match to win the Dorchester Trophy. After the match, he met homeless young people supported by the charity, and the organization received a check for £24,000 (approximately $36,000).[7]

SWIMMING

William is also an accomplished swimmer, a sport he shared with his mother from a very young age. Like Diana, William is fast in the water and has always enjoyed being in the pool. At seven, he won Wetherby's

Grunfield Cup for the best overall style. While a student at Eton, William excelled at many sports; however, it was in the pool where he truly excelled. As a junior, he won the 50-meter and 100-meter titles, and as a senior, he captained the school swimming team. He swam every day while in school, and when not at school, he swam at home, including using the pool at Buckingham Palace. At Eton, William also played water polo several times a week. So that he saw plenty of action in the game, and to utilize his physical prowess in the pool (he was six feet two inches at the time), he typically played the "up front" position. While at the University of St. Andrews, he represented the Scottish national universities' water polo team in the annual Celtic Nations tournament against Wales and Ireland.

FOOTBALL

Like many boys in England and in many other countries around the world, William developed an enthusiastic interest in football, or soccer as it is known in America, as a boy. As a student at Eton, William was immersed in his studies and in various activities, including playing games on the playing fields. Eton is known as a football school, and William was an enthusiastic and exceptional player, captaining his house's team, known as Gailey's team, in inter-house soccer matches. At St. Andrews, William played football regularly and joined Sunday league football for St. Salvator's Hall, his residence at university.

Throughout his life, William has been more than just an avid player and supporter of football. He is also the president of the English Football Association (FA), the governing body of the sport in Britain. As president of the FA, Prince William was a key supporter of the England 2018 World Cup bid. On June 5, 2010, William visited Wembley Stadium, the home field for the team, to meet the association and England 2018 staff and also spoke to members of the England team and the team's management already in South Africa for the 2010 World Cup games via a video-link. He said,

All the staff at Wembley and the players and management in South Africa are working so hard to make this a successful year

Britain's Prince William celebrates after scoring a goal during a training session as he visits the Football Association's Hat-Trick project at West Gate Community College, Centre for Sport, in Newcastle, England, October 18, 2007. (AP Photo/ Scott Heppell, Pool)

for English football. It could be a year of amazing achievement, on and off the field—we could win both the World Cup in South Africa and the World Cup vote in Zurich. It will certainly be tough but both are do-able . . . Winning both the World Cup and the Bid would be a huge boost to the whole country—and the whole country is behind them.

The general secretary of the FA, Alex Horne, said, "It was a great honour to host Prince William at Wembley. It was a real morale boost for everyone at the FA ahead of the World Cup and the England players and management really appreciated the message of support." The chief executive of England 2018, Andy Anson, said, "Prince William is one of our most important and effective advocates and he is totally committed to bringing the World Cup to England. He made that clear to our team and everybody was really motivated by his visit."[8] Unfortunately,

England lost its match to Germany in its quest for the World Cup Championship in June 2010.

RUGBY

In March 1991, William visited Cardiff, Wales, with his mother and brother. Diana wanted both her sons to learn more about the country whose name was part of their own titles. After visiting there, Diana became the unofficial mascot of the Welsh Rugby team and one of its biggest supporters. When she attended the international matches at Cardiff's Millennium Stadium, she brought William and Harry along. As a result of their early visits to Wales and watching the team with their mother, an avid supporter, William's interest in the sport came early. At one official competition, William and Harry were presented with badges by the Welsh Rugby Union, which they both wore proudly on their lapels. At Eton, William played rugby for the school's team until a hand injury in 1998 curtailed his playing.

Even though he cannot compete in the sport any longer, William has continued to love the game and follows international competitions. He shares an enthusiasm for rugby with his aunt, the Princess Royal, who is a royal patron of the Scottish Rugby Union, and though she and William share a passion for the sport, they have a friendly rivalry. She, of course, is a fan of the Scottish team, and William is a fan of the Welsh team. The Queen is currently the royal patron of the Welsh Rugby Union, and William is the vice royal patron.

In November 2007, in his capacity as the vice royal patron, William attended the world championship game between the Welsh team and the Springboks of South Africa team at the Millennium Stadium in Cardiff. At the conclusion of the game, he handed the inaugural cup, named in his honor, to South Africa. He said the creation of the Prince William Cup, to be played for every time the two nations meet, was a "privilege" and added that he hoped it would forge closer links between the two countries. Writing in the game's official program, Prince William said he was "honoured" to be present at the match. He wrote, "It is an enormous privilege to be involved in the Welsh Rugby Union's initiative to forge closer relationships between two proud rugby nations, both on the playing field and culturally." He added, "What a fine example of the two nations forging strong links with each other in order to broaden the horizons of those around them." A spokesman for the Royal Family said of William and the sport, "He is very keen to support rugby at all levels of the game throughout Wales."[9]

SKIING

William has enjoyed skiing for most of his life; he spent time on the slopes as a boy with both his parents and has skied as an adult with friends and family. Diana often took both William and Harry on skiing trips during school breaks. Prince Charles has always loved the sport as well and during most winters can still be found on the slopes at one of the many European resorts. William and Harry often joined their father on winter vacations, even though on most of their trips, there was a scheduled time of meeting reporters and photographers before the trio could take to the slopes. Because of their great love of the sport, winter vacations have always been important to the Royal Family.

It was in March 1991, when William was just eight years old, that he first learned to ski. Over a school break, Diana took William and Harry to Lech, an Austrian resort favored by the Dutch Royal Family. At the time, Charles and Diana were separated, and Charles, an avid and skilled skier, had first wanted to introduce his two sons to the sport; however, it was Diana who made arrangements to take them on a skiing holiday. Even without their father to teach them the mechanics of taking to the snow, both the princes enjoyed their first trip on skis. By the second day, Harry was more adventurous than his older brother and seemed to have no fear of taking tumbles down the slopes. William was a bit more cautious and found it a little more difficult to maintain a balance; he kept falling down. By the end of the week's vacation, William was proficient on skis and, in his typical enthusiasm for sport, was making his own way on the trails down the Austrian mountain.

The next year, during their Easter break from school, Charles and Diana were together long enough to take their sons on a second skiing holiday, again at the Lech resort. Unfortunately, the news that Diana's father had died came at the beginning of the holiday. The boys took the news in stride, as often happens with children just nine and seven years of age. Diana, believing that the boys' vacation should continue, left the resort to attend to her family while Charles stayed with the boys on the slopes. On their second time on the slopes, the two princes had a great competition of who could ski the fastest in a slalom race, and William's skills had improved enough that he beat his younger brother, who had seemed more of a natural skier from the first time he put on his skis. In 1994 and 1995, as Charles and Diana's marital difficulties continued, William had two skiing holidays, one with Charles at his favorite Swiss resort, Klosters, and another with Diana at Lech in Austria.

In March 1998, just six months after Diana's death, William, Harry, and Charles visited Canada. After attending official engagements in and around Vancouver, they went to Whistler for a private skiing holiday. Upon arriving in Canada, William was treated as a rock star. At Whistler, he was greeted with mobs of teenage girls carrying posters that showed their great affection for him. At first, the shy prince was uncomfortable, but he soon relaxed and even cheerfully accepted Harry's ribbing. Attired in designer jacket and cap provided by the popular and trendy Canadian sportswear company, Roots, William looked like a rock star too, or even a "super-royal"; his popularity as a member of the Royal Family was not known until then.

After spending Christmas at Sandringham with the Royal Family, William celebrated the New Year in 2006 with a skiing holiday. He had graduated from St. Andrews and was scheduled to enter Sandhurst, Britain's military academy. He had been dating Kate Middleton, and she had already spent time with members of the Royal Family, but she had not been invited to spend Christmas with William. So to spend time together, the couple ostensibly made plans to ski at one of their favorite holiday destinations, Verbier in Switzerland. However, the plans were actually a ruse devised to help them avoid reporters. The palace told reporters that William and Kate would go to Verbier, but instead, they were some 200 miles away in Klosters, where they spent their days skiing and their nights alone in a small chalet. Both accomplished skiers, William and Kate skied off-trail to try the powder atop Casanna Alp, a risk the royal protection officers deemed unacceptable. After they made their run together, they paused and kissed. Unfortunately for the couple, they had not realized the press had caught up with them, and the next day, the first photo of William and Kate kissing was everywhere, alongside the headline, "Kiss Me Kate."[10]

A ROYAL BIRTHDAY PARTY AT A DUDE RANCH IN MONTANA

Diana always made William and Harry's birthdays very special, and their parties were planned to great detail. When William turned 10, his party had a cowboys and Indians theme, and he and Harry dressed in cowboy outfits, and Diana dressed like Doris Day in the movie *Calamity Jane*. Charles was an honorary American Indian chief and was dressed in an Indian outfit, complete with a feathered headdress. Even though his parents were separated, Charles and Diana agreed to get through the party without fighting and joined in all the games. The cowboy theme continued later in the summer of 1992, when William joined a school friend and his family in Montana at the E-Bar-L dude ranch. The day began with a tin cup of tea and a bowl of porridge served from a chuck wagon. After a day of riding, swimming, fishing, and square dancing, William joined in on a hay ride into the surrounding hills. Out among the pine trees, he displayed his talent for clay pigeon target shooting. One of the cowhands employed at the ranch noted, "He didn't make a big thing of who he was. He was really friendly to the other kids. Even though he could ride and shoot better than most of the adults he wasn't big-headed about that either. He enjoyed passing on his skills." William telephoned his mother at home and said, "This is the best holiday of my life."[11]

William has always had a great love of competition, and even though he briefly considered at one time to take his accomplished riding and polo skills to a higher competitive level, he knew his participation in any sport would cause a great deal of attention, something he detests. He understands, however, that the attention is something he will always have to manage. Competing in sports will be his outlet, just as it has been throughout his life, and just as it has been for his father and many other royals throughout history. One of his contemporaries at Eton and at St. Andrews described William's sporting prowess this way: "He is totally without fear. If he has one fault, it is that he jumps in without thinking about the consequences. . . . he has perfect balance, and that, combined with a powerful physique, means he can play at contact sport . . . and give as good as he gets. He is a natural leader . . . he loves being captain of any team he plays in. He is not so good at taking orders."[12]

NOTES

1. Ingrid Seward, *William and Harry* (New York: Arcade, 2003), 45–46.

2. Christopher Andersen, *After Diana* (New York: Hyperion, 2007), 108.

3. Ingrid Seward, *William and Harry* (New York: Arcade, 2003), 262.

4. Brian Hoey, *Prince William* (Phoenix Mill, England: Sutton, 2003), 143.

5. Ingrid Seward, *William and Harry* (New York: Arcade, 2003), 245–46.

6. Tusk Trust, http://www.tusk.org (accessed June 24, 2010).

7. Centrepoint, http://www.centrepoint.org.uk (accessed June 24, 2010).

8. The Football Association, http://www.thefa.com (accessed June 28, 2010).

9. Prince of Wales Web site, http://www.princeofwales.gov.uk (accessed June 26, 2010).

10. Christopher Andersen, *After Diana* (New York: Hyperion, 2007), 263.

11. Ingrid Seward, *William and Harry* (New York: Arcade, 2003), 140–41.

12. Brian Hoey, *Prince William* (Phoenix Mill, England: Sutton, 2003), 144.

Chapter 7

A MOST ELIGIBLE BACHELOR, A DASHING GROOM

For a king or queen, whether the current sovereign or a future heir, there are many duties. Among them are drawing attention to causes, raising money for charities, opening exhibitions, advising Parliament, making speeches, bestowing titles, shaking hands with subjects, and posing for photographs. Yet there is only one required duty, and that is to marry a proper partner and produce an heir, for that is what impacts the future of a monarchy and the succession of the sovereigns' reign.

The selection of a suitable bride or groom to become the prince or the princess and thereby the future king or queen is not taken casually. Of course, today's world is far different for this important process. In prior generations, the future heir would marry according to the politics of the day and not for love. Marriages would often be arranged between dynasties so that alliances could be made, or they might have been arranged between not-so-distant relatives. Love may have been part of the arrangement, or the two may have grown to love each other, but this was not at all the norm. As long as an heir was produced, the relationship had little consequence. The history of the failures of many of these marriages weighs heavily on today's future king, for the consequences have often been disastrous for the monarchy. Over time, the monarchy has been in crisis and nearly in collapse.

William has gone from the traditional to the modern in many aspects of his life. These contradictions have been evident in his social life, with regard to whom he has dated and socialized with. He has been linked with supermodels, pop stars, and the daughters of politicos and government leaders. His flirting, real or imagined, has been splashed across newspapers and has led to gossip and rumors. William is a sensitive, private man, and although he loves the hunt and the shoot, he also loves partying with friends at home and at clubs, and he remains camera-shy and fiercely protective of his private life. He is well aware that he must embrace a public life and that his life is an open book, always on display with the potential of everything on the front page. He is also aware that his duty makes his own life a sacrifice to the realm he serves, yet he is a man who denies that his own needs and wants must be at the expense of his duty as a royal and his place as the future sovereign. His private life sometimes has been the reverse of his public life, and these contradictions, of partying and craving privacy, sometimes at the same time, have appealed to the opposite sex.

As a teenager, he was without a doubt a pinup idol for millions of teenage girls around the world. Prince William's heartthrob status began in 1982, when his country celebrated the birth of the future king. As a young boy, wherever he went, he attracted attention; he was beautiful, as many boys are, yet he was special even without being second in line to the throne. He had his mother's looks, blue eyes, blonde hair, and shy smile, which made people love him because they loved her; he also possessed a certain mischief that endeared him to millions. His emergence as a teen heartthrob began in 1995 when the British music magazine *Smash Hits* published a poster of him. Dressed in a school blazer, grey pants, dress shirt, and tie, young William, at just 13, was an instant hit with the girls, and the magazine sold out quickly. Girls who swooned over the young prince wrote him love letters, sending him their pictures and little gifts. And over the course of several Valentine's Days, he went from receiving 54 cards to more than 1,000. Another magazine gave away stickers that read "I Love Willy."[1]

In November 1997, when he was 15, he attended an anniversary party for the Queen and the Duke of Edinburgh, and more than 600 screaming teenage girls greeted him. In March 1998, when he was visiting Canada, the lovesick girls there gave him a pop star's welcome; they swooned, burst into tears, and pursued him as he skied the slopes. One screaming girl was overly thrilled: "Look at him! I've got posters of him all over my wall!" Another screamed, "They should declare it a national holiday, William Day!" At the time, with his bashful smile, so like his late mother's, he did his best to show the proper resolve expected of him at such a tender age. He shook hands and accepted gifts, his smile never leaving his face.[2] And when he solemnly walked behind his mother's coffin in 1997, he broke many hearts as people throughout the world watched him and mourned with him. When William became a teenager, what was dubbed "Willsmania" began.

Just like his father before he married Princess Diana, William has been considered one of the most eligible bachelors in the world. When Charles married Diana, he was 32; in 2010, William turned 28 and had once said he would not marry until he was at least 28, if not 30. Whether he has enjoyed the attention of being one of the most eligible bachelors in the world is only a guess. He is still shy, reserved, and very conscious of his duty and responsibilities as a future king. He is also fully aware of the consequences if he missteps; after all, the media is ever-present, and a kiss-and-tell story in all the newspapers is not something he needs or wants. Yet William has been known to love to party, and with all the beautiful women who tend to be wherever he is, at clubs, at social events, at polo matches, or at any other kind of venue, he could easily have his choice, with a relationship in mind or not.

Charles has always been quite open-minded about William's social life and has encouraged him to invite his friends to Highgrove or to St. James's Palace, taking the view that an open attitude to William's relationships is more sensible and may lessen the potential pitfalls inherent to anyone as famous and as eligible as his son. William has been well aware that any serious relationship would have to pass the muster of the palace and that, based on the marriages that have ended in divorce, including that of his own parents, it is essential that he find the "right" woman and that she be fully aware of what life will be like for her and for them together. As well, the Queen always made it known that she deems the choice of a wife for William as of the utmost importance in the continuity of the monarchy. William has always known that whomever he chooses would have to be acceptable to the Queen, and that the selection process would be extremely important. He has also been fully aware of what his bride, the princess and his future queen would face. It is obvious that William remains scarred by the violent death of his mother and still believes that she was hounded to her death by the paparazzi. He saw his mother terrorized and reduced to tears and how she had to use the press as much as avoid it to get through her life as the fairy-tale princess. His wariness of the press applies to all aspects of his life, including his protectiveness of his friends and certainly a future wife.

The selection of a suitable wife for William was an ongoing process for several years. At Buckingham Palace, files have long been prepared on prospective young women, and close watch was kept to see if any of them could emerge as a future bride and thereby the future queen. Although William fully understands that his duty is paramount and that it comes before his own personal happiness, he has questioned why it is so very vital that the obvious sacrifices made by his grandmother and even his father should still apply to him, especially in the world that has changed so drastically since his grandmother's ascension to the throne in 1952. He has seen other European monarchies make successful marriages without the marriage needing to be "suitable" to the monarchy. William wanted the selection of a wife to be his own choice and for his family and his country to have confidence in his ability to make his own suitable choice. William knew all along that when the time came for him to announce his engagement, it would be to someone his own age, someone he has known for some time, and likely someone not from an aristocratic background. However, he was well aware that both she and her family would be thoroughly investigated, and only when the palace was satisfied would the engagement be acceptable. These were the rules, and William would abide by them, even though he may have wished they were different.

THE WOMEN IN THE PRINCE'S LIFE

At the same age as most young men, while he was a student at Eton, William discovered girls. In October 1995, when he was 13, he asked for tickets to the Fiesta Ball at London's Hammersmith Palais, an annual event for the socially elite teenager. Charles and Diana agreed, and William attended the event with Eton school friends. Girls lined up to dance with the prince, and several of his pals had to act as bodyguards to shield him from their overly delighted behavior. The following year, when he was 14, he went skiing at Klosters, Switzerland, and spotted a teenage girl on the slopes. After skiing with her, he invited her to lunch. Later on the same trip, William was attracted to another young woman, and he invited her to ski with them. In 2000, he again visited Klosters, and he and Harry got together with 16-year-old Violet von Westenholz and her 13-year-old sister Victoria, daughters of former Olympic skier Piers von Westenholz. Later that year, at the Beaufort Polo Club, William enjoyed the company of model Natalie Hicks-Lobbecke, then 22, who is related to one of Germany's wealthiest aristocratic families.[3]

For William, being seen with any young woman has always raised speculations about whether she was a serious contender for his heart, sending the rumor mill into overdrive. When he turned 18, there were rumors that he was dating singer Britney Spears, which he said was utter nonsense. For years, William was seen with many young women, some he met at school, Eton or St. Andrews, and some he met on the polo field or on the ski slopes, two sports that attract beautiful women. There were never any firm indications that any of the women were girlfriends. Of course, William was very protective of his privacy, and parties and dates took place where the media could not be present, such as the cottage on the Balmoral estate, the homes of the parents of the girls he was with, his apartment at St. James's Palace, or Highgrove, all secure and safe places. For William, taking a young woman out to dinner or meeting for a drink clearly was not an option; there was always at least one bodyguard present, and the press would get word and descend immediately.

Over the years, the list of young women who have been seen with William has read like a social and aristocratic register. Prior to entering St. Andrews, he was linked with Arabella Musgrave, whose father manages the Cirencester Park Polo Club, where William often plays. In 1999, he was joined on a cruise of the Greek Isles by several young women, including Davina Duckworth-Chad, whose brother James is equerry (personal attendant) to the Queen and whose father was the former high sheriff of Norfolk, where he owns a 2,000-acre estate. He was also linked with Emma Parker Bowles, Camilla's niece. Also linked to the prince were Lady Katherine Howard, the daughter of the Earl of Suffolk, and Emilia d'Erlanger, a member of a special group invited to join him and Prince Charles on a Greek Isles holiday. There were likely others linked to William, some who may have met him only once, yet there was not a single name that ever emerged to eclipse all the others on William's list prior to university and during his first year at St. Andrews. However, what all the women linked to the prince had in common was that they were fiercely protective of him.[4]

When it was announced that William would attend St. Andrews in Scotland, inquiries and applications for admission increased significantly, and a great portion of the applicants were women; it seemed that young women wanted to study with the young prince. When he enrolled at the university, which has a reputation for wild parties, more than 4,000 admirers, mostly female, lined the streets of the small town of Fife to see him arrive. Many of the young women screamed at him, and four teenage girls in particular, who had traveled from Edinburgh to see him, squealed with delight when he quickly and coyly waved at them. Kirsten Taylor, 15 years old at the time, said, "We just wanted to see what he looked like in real life, and he's so beautiful. I think I know where we'll be spending some of our weekends in the future." The female students at the school had a way of "Wills spotting," as it was known. They kept each other up-to-date on his movements by text messaging each other.

At school in particular, William had to be careful about how he chose his friends. He had to be sure they wanted to know him because of who he was and not what his title was. Of course, many of the students attending Eton and St. Andrews were from the aristocracy or from wealthy and often famous families and thus were familiar with the protocol of how to behave and what was expected of them and the member of the Royal Family in their midst. William proved himself to be a very good judge of character and was able to choose well. He could sense when a person was genuine and worth knowing, regardless of his or her background, something he learned early on from his mother, who made sure both her boys treated everyone the same and understood there were people from all walks of life and all kinds of circumstance. When it came to girlfriends, there were, of course, many to choose from. Some threw themselves at him, and others knew better how they might get his attention.

Prince William is royal, rich, handsome, and charming. He is also unassuming, something that has made him different from so many others in the Royal Family and the aristocracy. Whether he was just William Wales, as he was called while in school, or Prince William of Wales, it was easy to attract attention and have a bevy of adoring women in the distance or close by. However, he has known he must be careful of the dangers of dating. Choosing the wrong woman could lead to the same disasters that have plagued so many of the Royals, including his parents. And he has understood clearly that any relationship he had, whether serious or casual, was likely going to be played out in the media. Not every woman would be able to accept, or want to accept, the inherent pressures that life with the prince would bring. When he marries Catherine "Kate" Middleton many women throughout the world will be sad, and others will sigh with relief that he is hopefully, happy. Because he has known Kate for so many years, and she knows his family, including the Queen very well by now, it is hoped she is ready and able to manage whatever being a princess and perhaps a future queen will bring.

A FUTURE KING'S DUTY IS TO MARRY

William has been linked to several women over the years, yet only one, Catherine (Kate, as she is familiarly known) Middleton, has often been by his side. Since his second year at St. Andrews, when he shared a flat with her and another student, William and Kate have been seen together, first as roommates and school friends and later as a couple. Their relationship has had its ups and downs, and it was reported over the years that they had split, but they always were seen together again later. Rumors of their relationship and potential engagement continued for several years, and odds were taken on whether Kate had won the Prince's heart.

After partying with friends and his brother, Prince Harry, at a favorite nightclub while on a ski vacation at Klosters in the Swiss Alps in March 2005, William sensed there might be embarrassing pictures in the newspapers the next day of a friend's party antics, so he signaled to his bodyguards that he would like to speak with the royal reporter for London's newspaper *The Sun,* Duncan Larcombe. Although there was no direct question about William's love life, the reporter did ask William about the latest picture taken of him and Kate Middleton as they skied together and then kissed on the slopes. William said he was genuinely surprised at the interest in the pictures. The reporter answered that there was much speculation that the relationship could lead to marriage and that an engagement would be announced soon. To this seemingly casual remark, William gave a frank answer: "Look, I'm only 22, for God's sake. I am too young to marry at my age. I don't want to get married until I am at least 28 or maybe 30."[5] Kate was standing nearby, and if she was disappointed by William's answer, she didn't show it. Perhaps she knew exactly what William was doing with the reporter. After all, she knew William very well, and they already had a long-term relationship, sometimes as friends, other times as a couple.

Not long after the strong statement from the prince about what the future held in the matter of marriage, a senior source revealed to author Robert Jobson, "The prince knew exactly what he was doing; he would not open his heart about his private life to a reporter he barely knows . . . without thinking about it first. It was for show; a way of dampening down speculation about him and Kate; a way of protecting her from the press."[6] For William, protecting his friends, and certainly his girlfriend, Kate Middleton, from the press was extremely important. He wanted to ensure that his friends were kept as safe and as far from the elements of the press as possible. There is no denying that William remains wary of the press and wants at least some of his life private. That has included when and whom he will marry.

The Queen has always taken a particular interest in William's romances and in his longtime relationship with Kate Middleton. As William has continued to prepare to be king, preparation that includes selecting a bride who will one day be queen, recent history has provided some lessons on this important process. It was William's great-great-uncle, King Edward VIII, who abdicated the throne in 1936 after declaring he could not be king if he could not have the woman he loved be queen, a divorced American woman deemed not acceptable to be the queen. There also was his parents' marriage, which dissolved so publicly and scandalously. The Queen wants to ensure, as much as possible, that any and all public scandals be avoided. William's marriage must be one that will last, one that is acceptable, and one that will not cause the monarchy embarrassment. William must get his marriage right the first time and not follow his father, who was said to be in love with Camilla but married Diana instead. When their marriage fell apart so publicly, the damage to the monarchy was swift and sure, and the embarrassment to the Queen was also very clear. What if it all happened again? The world is clearly different now than it was for William's parents and certainly for his great-great-uncle, but it has remained William's solemn duty to find a woman who is respectable and suitable, who will produce an heir, and who is prepared for the public life of a royal—a task that certainly is not easy and that carries the weight of the history of his country.

CATHERINE "KATE" MIDDLETON—A LADY IN WAITING

After Diana's death, William continued his studies at Eton, determined to move on and also wanting to return to a place where he was somewhat shielded from the press and the continued speculations about the circumstances of her death. He and his brother insisted that their mother would want them to move on with their lives. As time went on, William emerged from his mother's shadow; he worked hard at school, competed in sports, and earned Eton's Sword of Honour, the school's highest award for a first-year cadet. He was also in the midst of what became known as "Wills Mania," a heartthrob to girls who put posters of the young prince on their bedroom walls. And even though she later denied it, Kate Middleton was said to be one of those girls. As a student at the Marlborough School, some 30 miles from Eton, Kate reportedly pinned photographs on her dormitory wall.

Catherine Middleton, known as Kate, is the eldest of three siblings and was born on January 9, 1982, five months before William. She was raised, along with her sister Pippa and a brother, James, with strong family values and an expectation of a comfortable standard of living. Her father, Michael, is from an old Yorkshire family that dates back to the 16th century. According to a royal genealogist, one of the lines of Kate's father's side of the family descends from a family of solicitors related to John Thomas Hobbs, a royal marine and a great personal friend of King William IV. Her mother, Carole, is a former flight attendant. By the time Kate was six years old, her parents were on their way to building a fortune in a mail-order business called Party Pieces, a company that specializes in children's party supplies.

As a little girl growing up in Bucklebury, a small village in Berkshire, Kate dressed up in princess gowns and tiaras before they were shipped off to customers. A mother of one of Kate's childhood friends said, "At the time I remember Kate in her sparkly princess dress and little rhinestone crown, watching Princess Diana on the television and imitating her. Of course, all the little girls wanted to be Diana."[7]

After attending Downe House, an exclusive girls' boarding school in Berkshire, Kate enrolled at the Marlborough College, an elite coed boarding school, when she was 14. According to one of her friends, Gemma Williamson, Kate was "self-contained" and modest while at Marlborough, and Kate had arrived at the school suddenly in the middle of the school year, appearing thin and pale after a difficult experience at her previous boarding school. She added that Kate had very little confidence and that it did not help that the boys at the school had a system of "rating" new girls as they came into supper by holding up paper napkins with marks from 1 to 10 written on them. Kate scored only ones and twos when she arrived; however, one summer later, her scores were much higher. By the next year, Kate had filled out, color had returned to her cheeks, and she was "totally different." Gemma said, "Every boy in the school fancied her rotten." However, Kate was not terribly interested in the attention, believing she wanted to wait for someone special. Marlborough School, like many schools of its kind, was populated by the privileged children of wealthy and often absent parents. And, like many schools, it had its fair share of wild teenage behavior, with drinking, smoking, and flirtations that turned into sexual adventures. However, this was all lost on Kate. According to another good friend, Jessica Hay:

> She didn't have any serious boyfriends at school. She is very good-looking and a lot of boys liked her but it just used to go over her head. She didn't get involved in any drinking or smoking but was very sporty instead and very family-oriented. One of Cath-

erine's [Kate's] best assets is that she has always been very sure of herself. She has never allowed herself to be influenced by others and there is no way that she would be involved in any of that. She still doesn't really drink and certainly doesn't smoke. You're much more likely to find her going for a long walk across the moors than going to a nightclub. We would sit around talking about all the boys at school we fancied but Catherine would always say, 'I don't like any of them.' Then she would prophetically joke, 'There's no one quite like William.' When looking at the picture of William and his father fishing that was pinned to her wall, she would say that William looked kind; you could tell that, she said, just by looking at him. Her friends always said that one day she would meet him and they would be together.[8]

Who knew that it would all come true?

Like William, Kate set her sights on further studies at St. Andrews. William intended to study the history of art, geography, and anthropology, Kate also planned to study the history of art and spent her gap year in Florence, where she could see many of the art treasures that would fill her textbooks at university. While in Florence, besides immersing herself in the study of art, Kate also spent time enjoying a relaxed lifestyle with friends. Although many of her friends enjoyed the parties and indulgences available in the beautiful city, Kate demonstrated her by-now well-known self-control. She passed on drugs and excessive alcohol yet was never judgmental and at the same time was never considered too prim; she was not unpopular with friends or ridiculed because of her moral compass. Instead, she charmed those she met. One fellow student noted that the Italian barmen loved her, and because they fancied her, the rest of the young women would get free drinks. The Italians were charmed by her beauty and her "English rose appeal." Despite their continued attentions, Kate never encouraged them, perhaps because she had her sights set on different things and different people altogether.[9]

It had long been thought that William would follow his father and attend Trinity College, Cambridge. Instead, he chose to study at St. Andrews, where he believed he would have at least some privacy. Kate had long planned on attending St. Andrews. Little did she know her dream of meeting William would come to fruition very soon. As a "fresher," as first-year students are called, William settled into a residence hall, with his Scotland Yard personal protection officer next door. On another floor of the same hall, Kate also settled into her room. Many at St. Andrews were from the aristocracy with trust funds and expensive attire. Kate was financially comfortable; however, was not one of the trust-fund elite. She also was not from the group of students who attended the university on lesser family circumstances. From their first term, and despite their being from different social circles, Kate became a part of a small circle of friends that William established in hopes of maintaining privacy and having friends whom he could trust. He had declined to join the most elite and established campus social clubs, including a male-only club that everyone assumed he would join. When they met, they found commonality. Like William, Kate was a bit shy yet did not find it difficult to make friends. And like William, she loved sports. She skied, rode horses, played hockey, and enjoyed sailing. Besides being young and attractive, they had much in common and could talk to each other on many subjects, including each other's lives. It was easy for them to see each other because they lived in the same residence hall. Their times together did not have to be arranged and came more naturally, more spontaneously. They played tennis together and visited a bar they both enjoyed, and when William invited friends to his room for a drink, Kate often joined in. What may have naturally drawn William to Kate was her compassion and the fact that she made time for everyone. Of course, there was no denying her beauty.

William developed a strong friendship with Kate. In fact, she and William made a pact to stay at university together, even though both found it difficult to settle in, as many freshman college students do. Despite his friendships with Kate and others and the life he had structured at St. Andrews, William was not happy and considered changing schools, or even quitting the four-year program altogether. The palace and Charles, however, had other plans; they did not want William to appear to be a quitter. Charles strongly advised William to stay at St. Andrews. His grandfather told him to "just get on with it." He also was seeing other young women, and before arriving at university, he had a relationship with Arabella Musgrave, a 21-year-old who shared his love of polo. The relationship ended so that William could concentrate on his university studies, yet he found himself not wanting to be away from her and made weekend trips to Highgrove, hundreds of miles away from school in Fife, Scotland, to see her. Some suggested that Arabella was his first "true" love. When he attempted to reconnect with her in 2002, he decided a long-distance romance could not work. Despite ending their relationship, they remained good friends.

At the time that William was considering leaving university, Kate was having her own set of doubts. She was struggling with the transition from school to university and was making tearful calls home. Comparing notes, William and Kate shared their troubles, and each became a confidant for the other. Kate encouraged William to change his course of study from the history of art to geography, a subject in which he had always been interested. After switching his studies, he felt happier. As he felt better about university life, his social life picked up too. He decided to join the all-male club known as the Kate Kennedy dining club, and Kate became a member of the female equivalent, the Lumsden Society. Their friendship deepened as their small group of friends enjoyed meals together and made trips together. Kate became known to the public by her friendship to the future king. In April 2002, the press published pictures of her strutting down a student catwalk for a charity fashion show, sponsored by Yves Saint Laurent. William, having paid £200 for a front row seat, was mesmerized as he watched her model a black lace dress over a bandeau bra and black bikini bottoms. A fellow student had tipped off *The Mail on Sunday* newspaper, and the story ran under the headline "William and His Undie-Graduate Friend Kate to Share a Student Flat." The student said of William and Kate, "Kate was the real reason behind William's decision to go [to the fashion show]. She is one of a group of really good mates he has who all hang out together and have helped him through the past few months . . . they are strictly friends, there's absolutely nothing more in it than that." Although he had been ready to leave St. Andrews a month before, after a heartfelt talk with Kate, he not only was staying but also had begun looking for a flat to share with friends, including Kate.[10] Although Kate had been a friend before, now she seemed to be on everyone's radar screen.

When William was set to begin his second year at St. Andrews, he moved out of the residence hall and into an apartment in a Victorian-style home located on one of the more posh streets in town, with Kate and a fellow Etonian, Fergus Boyd. A personal protection officer also shared the flat. One friend said of Kate and William, "They get on really well. She is a very lovely girl but very unassuming . . . also discreet and loyal to William." Another said, "She treats him just like any other student. A lot of girls, especially the Americans, follow him round like sheep and he hates that. He just wants to live with people knowing he can be himself. He just wanted to live with Kate."[11] At the time, William and Kate were thought to be good friends and not romantically linked. Kate already had a boyfriend and was soon torn. She and William had long talks and shared confidences, and after that time together, she had other thoughts about William. Soon, their friendship was obviously something more. Yet they kept their relationship quiet. Their flatmates supported them, and William and Kate agreed to refrain from any public displays of affection. The charade worked well, even though they were a couple by the spring of 2002. As much as a year later, Kate's own father was unaware of the romance: "I can categorically confirm that they are no more than just good friends. . . . They are together all the time because they're the best of pals . . . But there is nothing more to it than that. We are very amused at the thought of being in-laws to Prince William, but I don't think it is going to happen."[12]

Just after her father denied the relationship, Kate turned 21 and celebrated with a party in her parents' home. Friends came to toast with champagne and enjoy a sit-down dinner, with everyone dressed, at Kate's request, in 1920s fashions. Slipping in unannounced was William. The two began talking and relaxing together, and then William had to leave, likely wanting to remain discreet. As flatmates and fellow students, William and Kate enjoyed partying with friends in Edinburgh and London, and on weekends and holidays, the couple often went to Balmoral, where both William and Harry had the use of a refurbished three-bedroom cottage, complete with four fireplaces and a staff of six.

Kate was secure in her relationship with William and was able to ignore the women who continued to flock around him. When William turned 21, he decided how he would celebrate his coming-of-age with a party at Windsor Castle. After visiting Africa during his gap year, he had remained enamored by the country and its people. For his party, he chose an "Out of Africa" theme, and the Queen approved. William wore a yellow and black striped loincloth, and the

Queen was dressed as the Queen of Swaziland, in a white sheath dress, a white fur wrap, and an African headdress. Charles wore a striped kaftan, and Harry, Prince Philip, and Prince Andrew were all dressed in safari wear. The guests enjoyed elephant rides, and monkeys swung from the palm trees imported for the event. William entertained his guests by playing African drums with a Botswanan band. All eyes, it seemed, were on the dark-haired woman who had a place of honor beside William. With Kate's blessing, William had invited his past girlfriend, Jessica (Jecca) Craig, who had been more than a friend to the prince when he visited Kenya, to be his guest of honor. A royal spokesperson quickly quashed any ideas of a romance and issued a public denial. Staying close to their friends from St. Andrews, Kate kept a low profile at the party, just as William had a few months before when she had celebrated her own 21st birthday party at her parents' house in Berkshire.

William was also known for partying in clubs in London, and young women were known to gather around him, hoping to get close enough to at least dance with the dashing prince. Very few of these women who were able to get close to the prince were as discreet as Kate Middleton. Sometimes William would sit in a corner or in specific sections set aside for the rich and famous and drink with friends. Other times, he was known to enjoy himself a bit more and get up on the dance floor. In September 2003, William visited a popular club called Purple and spent the evening dancing and necking with a young woman whose mother went public with her daughter's story, saying, "She [her daughter] would like to see him again because she really, really enjoyed his company. And if it happens, well, we'll just see." Needless to say, it did not happen. In October 2003, William spent an evening at the same club with a 29-year-old single mother. When she found out a week later that William and Kate Middleton were purportedly a couple, she told one tabloid that "William has too much of a roving eye to ever settle down. The way he acted with me he didn't seem to be in love with anyone else. He also chatted with a dancer and eyed up a girl in the VIP area. You wouldn't have guessed he was seeing Kate. Wills looked very much on the prowl, so Kate better watch out if she doesn't want to be made a fool of." She added that William made no mention of having a girlfriend and that she wished Kate luck. Her warning, as well as other stories of William's flirtations, did not fall on deaf ears, and the next time he visited the same club, Kate went along.[13]

A RELATIONSHIP IN TROUBLE

William and Kate's relationship continued, and he seemed to be less obsessed about keeping it private. Kate was invited on skiing vacations to the Klosters, where pictures were taken of them close together on the slopes. They also vacationed together on the island of Rodrigues in the Indian Ocean, a place William had visited during his gap year. They snorkeled and went scuba diving among the coral reefs, explored the island on motorbikes, and joined friends for drinks in the evenings. They even had nicknames for each other; she was "Kat" or "Kitten," and he was "Big Willy." It seemed their relationship was growing more serious; however, after their summer vacation on the island, there was trouble between the couple when he made plans to visit Jecca Craig in Kenya. Despite his assurances that there was nothing between him and his past girlfriend, Kate asked William not to make the trip. One friend noted, "She felt threatened and humiliated. It was one thing to never be publicly acknowledged, but quite another to have someone else bandied about in the press as the woman in his life."[14] Although they were often seen together, and William was less obsessed about who saw them, it was unusual that they would be seen so openly having a fight about his upcoming Africa trip while sitting in the front seat of William's car. William relented and canceled his trip. A short time later, he was seen with Jecca at two weddings, and Kate was nowhere to be seen. As well, William was spending time with an American, Anna Sloan, who was also studying in Scotland. Not long after they met, Anna's father was killed in a shooting accident; the two were drawn together mostly because they each had lost a parent in such a violent way. In the late summer of 2004, William accepted her invitation to visit her in America. There for a week, William enjoyed his time lounging by the pool, going to movies, and visiting a local mall like many Americans his age. He also enjoyed not being immediately recognized.

Even though he had not gone to Africa to visit Jecca, his trip to Anna's home in America raised speculations that he and Kate were breaking up. Their relationship had bloomed in the relative seclusion offered by St. Andrews, but the price of this privacy and seclusion could sometimes be claustrophobic, especially to William. Their relationship had been made known to the public only a few months before, and now there were signs that it was crumbling. One report noted that the two had agreed to a separation, something more often associated with a married couple. In April 2007, a mutual friend confirmed that the two had agreed to "amicably" split up. The split shocked their friends, fans, and royal-watchers. This was the couple who seemed to have a story-book relationship. One of Kate's friends noted that Kate was handling it with her impeccable poise, her down-to-earth charm, and a princess-ready style: "[everyone says] how good Kate was for him, but I think they were good for each other, really. It's sad."[15]

One reason for their troubles may have been that the two were tired of being under the strain of their own public affair. William had at first insisted they conduct their relationship almost in secrecy, something nearly impossible to do. He then relented somewhat, and they were seen together more often. Contributing to the strains, their university studies were coming to an end, and their coursework was mounting, with finals rapidly approaching. William wanted to give his studies more attention, and although Kate had the same university stresses and workload, she was more troubled by William's plans to travel abroad once his studies ended. Instead of staying in Scotland between the time their final exams ended and their graduation ceremony, William wanted to travel on his own. As well, he was conscious that the end of his university life would bring on more responsibilities and duties, and he would be required to take the next steps that would include less privacy and more media attention. A senior palace source said the two had serious discussions about the future: "Prince William thinks the world of Kate Middleton but he has confided to at least one of his best friends that the relationship has been getting a little stale and he thinks they may be better suited as friends. He has been unhappy in the relationship for a while, but the last thing he wants is a high-profile split in the crucial months leading to his finals. The truth is he thinks that when they graduate in the spring they'll go their own ways."[16]

To anyone in a serious relationship, this pronouncement would be quite a blow. Their high-profile relationship had played out in the newspapers with pictures of a couple apparently in love. They had been skiing together and had spent a luxurious holiday together on a remote island, and their time together had been seemingly blissful. Now it seemed it was over. However, Kate understood William and his needs. She could have made demands or delivered ultimatums, yet she did not. She was confident, even though naturally upset. She was fearful that William was really attempting to extricate himself from their relationship, but she was said to have told him that she valued his friendship so highly that she was prepared to accept him wanting his own time and space. She even offered to move out of their flat. Kate was able to hold on, to understand, and to play it as cool as possible. She knew she could not be someone hanging on to William; she knew him well enough to understand this. She also understood the pressures he was under. For William, it was a difficult time. Those close to him pointed out that part of his anxiety came from his sense of his destiny. As the future king, he needed to do what duty demanded, and it was his duty to marry at some point. And he knew that once he reached a certain stage of intimacy with a woman, there was no turning back. He was also well aware that he had to make the "right" choice.

Kate gave William the time and space he needed, and later, their love rekindled in the Scottish Highlands at Balmoral. They traveled there together on at least three occasions, and in March 2005, the world saw their intimacy when William invited Kate to join him skiing at Klosters again on his father's annual family ski-break with his sons. William was attentive, and it seemed that he had eyes only for Kate on the trip. William was more relaxed than ever with Kate in public, even though there were still attempts to protect her from the press. Charles was very comfortable with Kate as well, and they were seen chatting over dinner or in deep conversation as they rode the gondola on the ski slopes. It was on this trip that Charles and Kate were photographed together for the first time, even though Charles had told reporters several months earlier that he thoroughly approved of William's choice of a partner. Both Charles and Camilla found her to be charming, and she was clearly at ease with William's family, including Harry, Harry's friends, and Harry's girlfriend, Chelsy Davy. After six months of the relationship potentially ending, or at least being on hold, the two were a couple again.

William graduated from St. Andrews on June 23, 2005. Attending the elaborate ceremony, where William, kneeling before the university chancellor, was tapped lightly on the head with a 17th-century cap that contained a scrap of cloth believed to be from the pants of the Protestant Reform leader John Knox, were the Queen, Prince Philip, Harry, Charles, and Camilla. A red and black academic hood, signifying his Master of Arts status, was then affixed to his collar, and he was handed his diploma. Also graduating that day, sitting with 80 graduates and five rows ahead of William, was Kate. Wearing high heels and a black miniskirt beneath her academic robes, she accepted her degree in the history of art, and when she glanced at William, the two exchanged broad smiles. As part of his speech to the graduates and their friends and family, the university vice chancellor said, "I say this every year to all new graduates: you may have met your husband or wife. Our title as 'Top Matchmaking University in Britain' signifies so much that is good about St. Andrews, so we can rely on you to go forth and multiply."[17] All eyes, especially those who had speculated about the couple for months, seemed to be on William and Kate. William grimaced, and Kate raised her eyebrows in mock horror.

As the ceremony ended, Clarence House, on William's behalf, issued an official thank you statement that read, "I have thoroughly enjoyed my time at St Andrews and I shall be very sad to leave. I just want to say a big thank you to everyone who has made my time here so enjoyable." William also said, "I have been able to lead as normal a student life as I could have hoped for and I am very grateful to everyone, particularly the locals, who have helped make this happen."[18] After the ceremony, William walked to the town police station, where he thanked the local policemen for looking after him. On his way, he was met with the noise of hundreds of people lining the streets, very much like when William first arrived at St. Andrews as a freshman student. He shook hands with many of the people cheering him on. He then joined his family and introduced Kate and her family to the Queen; they were at first reluctant, but William offered his encouragement. Kate's mother curtsied, and the Queen appeared to welcome them warmly. It appeared Kate had been accepted by the Queen and the Royal Family. She had by now been a part of William's life for nearly four years.

A TRIP TO AFRICA AFTER THEIR GRADUATION

William's mother, Diana, had once observed that young William was like a "caged lion" in the confines of London, with all the "stiff collars and buttoned-up life of the city." Now many years later, he found something irresistible and liberating in wide-open spaces, in Gloucestershire, near his father's Highgrove estate, in the bleakness of the moors at Balmoral in Scotland, or in the searing heat of Africa. It seemed natural that William would want to get away whenever possible, to escape the rigors of the life of a royal and to relieve some of the pressures and stress. So it was, after graduation from St. Andrews, that William and Kate went to Africa. The trip meant getting away from the pressures at home. Final exams were over, the graduation ceremony had gone well, and it was time to be together in a place that William loved; five years earlier, he had spent a month working on a ranch in Kenya as part of his gap year and had returned there nearly every year since. What was somewhat odd about the trip was that the couple stayed at the same ranch, known as Lewa Downs, owned by the parents of Jecca Craig, the woman to whom Kate had feared losing William a year earlier. In fact, it was Jecca who served as a tour guide for Kate and William and the friends who were also on the trip. Lewa Downs, settled by Jecca Craig's family in 1924; it was her home and now was considered a second home for William. The trip was exactly what William and Kate needed, time away in a place William loved and shared with friends. It was a place filled with the sounds of Africa, where they were near zebras at a watering hole, giraffes feeding on the high trees, and elephants and lions somewhere in the bush.

BACK IN ENGLAND

Upon their return to England, Kate was drawn more and more into the world of the Royals. She met with the Queen several times without William present and also dined with the Queen and William at Windsor Castle. It appeared that Kate was being continually assessed and was learning more about the family and the duties and responsibilities inherent to being a royal. She was also learning about the joys and the stresses and strains of being William's girlfriend. After leaving St. Andrews, where their privacy had been guarded, William and Kate found themselves in the spotlight. They both had become fair game to the press, and the agreements made with the editors of the press while they were students had ended.

William began to worry more about how to protect Kate from the media, and more specifically from the paparazzi that seemed to be constantly present. When they were together, his security detail provided a shield against intrusions by the press. They had lived together for three years at St. Andrews, but now William could stay with Kate at her flat in the Chelsea section of London only occasionally because it had to be repeatedly checked by Scotland Yard before he could stay there. However, there was nothing the police could do to protect Kate when she was out without the prince. There were always several photographers following her, whether she was out shopping or meeting friends. They hid behind cars or leapt from behind shrubs as she carried a bag of groceries into the back of her car. What she was experiencing was very reminiscent of what Diana had gone through before she married Charles, and William did not want this for the woman he loved. At first, Kate merely smiled and persevered, but William worried that she would, like his mother, feel hunted. Unfortunately, the issue of the press came to a head when, in late 2005, the German magazine, *Das Neue*, published photographs showing William leaving Kate's flat after spending the night there. A large red arrow pointed to the flat with the caption "The Love Nest." William fumed at what he called the irresponsibility of the newspaper in pointing to the exact location of Kate's flat, especially in light of potential terrorist attacks and the specific attack that had occurred on July 7, 2005, where 52 commuters were killed in London. The royal law firm sent a letter to the newspaper editors that warned their photographers to stay away from Kate. Charles advised William not to take any further legal action; however, William wanted to see if a ruling could be made that would ban the tabloid press from publishing photos of Kate, and he asked his lawyers to prepare to take her case for privacy to the European Court of Human Rights if the situation worsened. Charles disagreed with William's stand against the media and warned him that any court action might backfire. By the end of 2005, it was clear that Kate was still being pursued by the press, although she had lessened her exposure to the outside world by choosing to work at home. The story of the commoner known as Kate Middleton, who might someday be a royal bride, and even queen, filled the mainstream media and the tabloid press. The newspaper *Independent on Sunday* called Kate "Her Royal Shyness."[19]

William and Kate spent the New Year holiday at Klosters, to ski and be together in what was described as a modest chalet. They both knew they would be separated soon, once William entered Sandhurst, England's military academy, on January 8, 2006, to begin his yearlong training. Harry was already a cadet there, and now it was William's turn to begin training, all a part of his preparation as a future king.

With William away at Sandhurst, where his life was on a strict, rigid schedule, Kate had to carry on without him. It was a difficult time because she was well aware that anything she did or said could and would be spun into a news story. She was not one to sit and dream about a life with the prince; rather, she was someone who kept busy. A source close to the couple said about Kate, "She is not and never has been somebody who would rest on her laurels. But it is fair to say that this was a difficult period for both of them."[20] William had his route pretty much mapped out, but Kate, while all her life was being examined, despite the efforts to shield her from the press, seemed to be at loose ends. She considered working in an art gallery, using her university degree in art history. She also considered starting her own business while working part-time at her parents' business, Party Pieces.

In March 2006, Kate attended the Cheltenham Gold Cup Thoroughbred Races with friends, and without William. During the second race, she appeared with Charles and Camilla in the royal box. This was the first time she had been invited to appear at a royal official function on her own. To onlookers, she appeared at ease with the Prince of Wales, and there was an obvious rapport with Camilla, the Duchess of Cornwall, who was at the race for her most high-profile social engagement since marrying Charles. The pictures of that day at the races showed a potentially new kind of Royal Family. One observer said, "It was astonishing to see how relaxed and comfortable Kate was around the heir to the throne. It just goes to prove how serious her relationship with William is. It also shows how fond Camilla is of her too . . . she did not appear to be remotely put out at being overshadowed by Kate's presence." From her presence in the royal box that day, the bookmaker odds on Kate and William getting engaged before the following year's Cheltenham Gold Cup race went from 40–1 to 25–1.[21]

Kate's place within the Royal Family was obviously growing more secure. She had received the coveted invitation to the Royal Family's Christmas dinner at Sandringham, an invitation that many believed signaled her complete acceptance into the family. And even though she turned down the invitation, saying that a family dinner should be just for family and that she would spend Christmas with her own family instead, the invitation was a sign that she was William's chosen princess. Charles, in consultations with William's personal protection officers and Scotland Yard, gave his permission for a bodyguard to be hired to protect her. Charles also gave his permission for Kate and William to occupy the same room whenever she visited Highgrove. The Queen decided that the house William shared with Harry at Balmoral would be renovated, and she made the hideaway a gift to William and the woman she hoped would someday be his bride. Prince Charles continued with his plans to build an environmentally friendly, 8,500-square-foot stone mansion, stables, and chapel on the Duchy of Cornwall's Harewood Park Estate. The property would have six reception rooms and six bedroom suites and was intended for William once he married. The Queen had already set aside royal titles for William and his bride, whoever she might be; they would be known as the Duke and Duchess of Cambridge.

While apart, William and Kate sent each other text messages several times a day, and when he could away from his duties at Sandhurst, William was in London with Kate. Even though they had been apart for extended periods of time, to the royal subjects, William and Kate appeared to be a couple in love. To many, it seemed that it was not a matter of whether they would be married, but when they would be married. Kate was referred to as a princess-in-waiting, or lightheartedly as "Waity-Katie." Would she someday be Queen Catherine? It has always been clear that William is extremely protective of Kate, and the similarities between her and his mother do not go unnoticed; he does not want her to suffer through what his mother clearly endured when it came to the media, specifically the paparazzi.

To be sure, Kate Middleton's family is not aristocratic. She is a woman from an upper-middle-class family who happened to catch the eye of the man second in line to the throne. In the history of the monarchy, Kate is not someone who would have been considered princess material. In today's monarchy, she has passed all the tests; she has no lurid past, she has conducted herself with dignity, she has shown her loyalty to William and the Royal Family, and she has maintained great poise and maturity in a relationship that has played out in the media. Although William has been well aware that duty is paramount when choosing a bride, he is the product of his parents' stormy marriage, and being somewhat of a rebel and very much a product of today's world and its expectations, William has questioned whether, in a truly modern monarchy, the duty calls for such self-sacrifice as endured in past generations. He has believed that he should be allowed to make his own choice in his own time and that his family and his country should have confidence in his ability to do so.

THE ENGAGEMENT ANNOUNCEMENT AND PREPARING FOR "THE PEOPLE'S WEDDING"

"Kate is not joining the Windsor dynasty to be a princess, she's joining to be a queen at some point in the future. There's a lot at stake here, more than just pretty dresses and magazine covers. You have to show that the dynasty can renew and rejuvenate itself. She and William have to make sure this marriage works."— Patrick Jephson, former private secretary to Princess Diana[22]

Throughout history, long engagements have not been typical in the Royal Family. Before he was crowned King George VI, William's great-grandfather proposed to Elizabeth Bowes-Lyon several times before she finally accepted in January 1923; they were married in April that same year. Prince Philip proposed to the current Queen Elizabeth II in 1946; the engagement was kept secret until her father, King George VI, gave his permission for them to marry in April 1947. Prince Charles had been seeing Lady Diana Spencer for less than a year when he proposed marriage in early 1981; they were married in July 1981. William and Kate were good friends at first, and then they began dating more than eight years ago. After their many years as a couple, many believe it is time for them to be married, especially given that William is second in line to the throne. Supporters of the monarchy believe the Royal Family is in need of a youthful romance, a reminder of the fairy tale; still others who may want the two to marry do not believe the country should pay for another elaborate wedding in light of the country's difficult economic times. The monarchy, many say, needs to prove to its people that the Royal Family is relevant and that the monarchy should be maintained. Still, difficult times or not, a reminder of the fairy tale or not, a royal wedding would take many minds away from the difficult economy and provide an economic boost to the country from increased tourism, which many say is what the country needs.

After years of fevered anticipation, on Tuesday, November 16, 2010, after informing the Queen and Prince Charles, William and Kate announced their engagement at a brief press conference at St. James's Palace. With his arm locked to his fiancée's, William told the crowd of reporters and photographers that he had proposed while the two were visiting Kenya in October. He had given Kate his mother's engagement ring, an oval blue sapphire surrounded by diamonds, saying it was his way of making sure his mother did not miss out on the day and the excitement. Few were surprised by the news. The engagement was one of the safest bets in all of England, and the news, even at a time of economic uncertainty and cutbacks, was considered good news.

The Queen issued a statement announcing that she and Prince Philip were absolutely delighted by the news. Prince Charles said that he was thrilled and jokingly added that the two had been practicing long enough. Prime Minister David Cameron wished the couple great joy in their life together and said he remembered camping out on the street the night before Charles and Diana's wedding procession; he said he thought the royal wedding would be a great moment for national celebration that would unite Britain and added that when he announced the news during a cabinet meeting, it was greeted with cheers and "great banging on the table." Prince Harry, William's brother, said that he was delighted that his brother had popped the question and that it meant he would get the sister he had always wanted. Kate's parents, Carole and Michael Middleton, welcomed the prince to their family, saying that William was wonderful and that the two made a lovely couple. William's bride-to-be, always known informally as Kate, would

Britain's Prince William and his fiancée Kate Middleton arrive for a media photo call at St. James's Palace in London, November 16, 2010, after they announced their engagement. The couple are to wed in April 2011. (AP Photo/ Sang Tan)

now, the palace noted, go by the official name of Catherine and would, after the wedding, be known as Princess Catherine. Should William ascend to the throne, Catherine will be Queen Catherine Elizabeth. She will be the first queen in British history to have a college degree or, more precisely, to have any college education at all.

A week after the engagement announcement, Clarence House, the official London residence for Prince Charles, his wife Camilla, and William and Harry, announced that William and Catherine would marry at Westminster Abbey on Friday, April 29, 2011. An aide to Prince William said the couple had chosen the Abbey for its "staggering beauty" and because it offers intimacy despite its grand scale. Westminster Abbey has been a coronation church since 1066, when the Norman King William I was crowned. It is where the Queen's father was crowned King George VI in 1937; it is also where Queen Victoria was crowned in 1837 and the current queen was crowned in 1953. It is also the final resting place for 17 monarchs.

Westminster Abbey is a traditional royal wedding venue; the current queen, Queen Elizabeth II, and Prince Philip were married in the Abbey in 1947; the Queen's mother, the late Queen Mother, was also married in the Abbey in 1923. The Abbey was also the venue for Princess Diana's funeral in 1997.

Questions about the ceremony and all the festivities surrounding another royal wedding flourished after the announcement. What would Kate's dress look like? Would the ceremony be as elaborate as that of Prince Charles and Diana? How would Diana be remembered at the wedding?

With the couple reportedly "on cloud nine," they said they wanted their wedding to be as much for them as for the people. In their view, it was to be a party, and they wanted the wedding to be "classically British." Plans included having the wedding kick off a four-day celebration, with the wedding day being a bank holiday, followed by the traditional May Day bank holiday on the following Monday. With the couple keen on having the public involved in the celebrations, it was announced that a lottery would be held to invite 100 members of the public to their wedding via a random drawing. The lucky 100 guests will mix with more than 2,000 invited guests, including a host of international royals and heads of state; they will also attend the reception held at Buckingham Palace. St. James Palace also announced that in an effort to avoid piling the cost of the wedding onto taxpayers, and with William very conscious of Britain's precarious finances, the wedding expenses would be shared by the Royal Family, including the Queen and Prince Charles and Catherine's parents. The taxpayers, however, would have to foot the bill for security. "We'd be delighted. It would be madness for them not to get married. Kate's one of us—she doesn't put on airs and graces, and she's such a lovely girl. Everyone who meets her, likes her," said Pru Shepheard, doing her daily shopping at the village store where Kate is a frequent customer, occasionally accompanied by William, in Yattendon, England.[23]

Catherine, as princess, may well have the same impact and the same popularity as Diana, and she will, at least initially, be compared to Diana, who is still known as the people's princess and remains extremely popular. Catherine is older than Diana was when she married Charles, and she is described as mature, self-assured, and far better equipped to deal with the media attention than Diana. Although Charles and Diana hardly knew each other at the time of their engagement, Catherine and William have known each other for more than eight years. Catherine is described as intelligent and educated and has had the opportunity of formal training by the monarchy's press team. She has taken tea and dined with the Queen and has apparently been given the Queen's approval. Matthew Bell, the social reporter for the weekly magazine *The Spectator,* who relied on an unnamed palace source, wrote, "Not only has she gained the Queen's approval, but the Duke of Edinburgh is said to be especially fond of her, and Charles and Camilla already see her as part of the family."[24]

No one wants William's bride to suffer as Diana apparently suffered in her role as princess. No one wanted to see William rush into a marriage that would prove to be as miserable as that of his parents. His choice for a bride was extremely important and one that he wanted to make on his own. His choice is clearly Catherine Middleton and evidently has been his choice since their days at university, and she has also been chosen by the Queen, who has deemed her suitable and, to all appearances, likeable. Their engagement has moved from the gossip columns to the palace agenda. She is considered a royal now, even before their marriage ceremony, and she is experiencing some of the perks that come with that role, as well as enduring many of its drawbacks. Her role in the life of the future sovereign is assured. Since they rented their flat with friends at St. Andrews in 2002, their relationship has blossomed into an intimate, stable one. They have weathered difficult times and have supported each other. In their time together, they both have emerged into responsible, mature, confident adults. Catherine has entered a world that must have at one time seemed like a fairy tale, and yet she has filled her role thus far with great style and confidence. Her days as a princess, and very likely as a future queen, have now begun.

NOTES

1. Tim Graham and Peter Archer, *William* (New York: Atria Books, 2003), 192.

2. Robert Jobson, *William's Princess* (London: John Blake, 2006), 66, 67.

3. Tim Graham and Peter Archer, *William* (New York: Atria Books, 2003), 198.

4. Brian Hoey, *Prince William* (Phoenix Mill, England: Sutton, 2003), 155.

5. Robert Jobson, *William's Princess* (London: John Blake, 2006), 3.

6. Ibid., 5, 6.

7. Christopher Andersen, *After Diana* (New York: Hyperion, 2007), 152, 153.

8. Robert Jobson, *William's Princess* (London: John Blake, 2006), 92, 93.

9. Ibid., 96, 97.

10. Ibid., 121, 122.

11. Ibid., 123.

12. Christopher Andersen, *After Diana* (New York: Hyperion, 2007), 154.

13. Robert Jobson, *William's Princess* (London: John Blake, 2006), 130.

14. Christopher Andersen, *After Diana* (New York: Hyperion, 2007), 214.

15. Simon Perry et al., "Separate Ways," *People,* April 30, 2007, 96–103.

16. Robert Jobson, *William's Princess* (London: John Blake, 2006), 140.

17. Ibid., 159.

18. Ibid., 158.

19. Christopher Andersen, *After Diana* (New York: Hyperion, 2007), 259.

20. Ibid., 192.

21. Ibid., 201.

22. Gregory Katz, "Prince William, Kate Middleton Royal Wedding?" *Huffington Post*, November 12, 2010.

23. Ibid.

24. Robert Mason Lee, "William Takes a Bride?" *Maclean's*, August 15, 2005, 40–41.

Chapter 8

THE PRINCE'S MILITARY CAREER

FOLLOWING IN HIS PARENTS' FOOTSTEPS IN PHILANTHROPY AND HUMANITARIANISM

The last thing I want to do is to be molly-coddled or be wrapped up in cotton wool, because if I was to join the army, I would want to go where my men went, and I'd want to do what they did. I would not want to be kept back for being precious, or whatever—that's the last thing I would want.

—Prince William

Throughout the history of the monarchy, kings and queens alike have had strong connections with the military; they either have directly served or have been the guide and inspiration for their country's mighty armies and navies in times of war and peace. The first sovereigns were often military commanders, leading fighting forces into battle and fighting alongside their armies. For example, in 1066, King Harold died on the battlefield after being hit by an arrow and then struck by the sword of a knight. Another example was William I, also known as William the Conqueror, who took over and directed the troops and continued the fighting.

Over time, battles were waged without the sovereign in the midst of the warfare. Instead, the rulers left the fighting to their experienced commanders. Such was the case for Queen Elizabeth I; although she did not directly command her armies on the battlefield, she was their inspiration. In 1588, on the eve of the Spanish Armada, the Queen addressed her armies in a rousing speech: "I know I have the body of a weak, feeble woman; but I have the heart and stomach of a king—and of a King of England too, and think foul scorn that Parma or Spain, or any prince of Europe, should dare to invade the borders of my realm; to which, rather than any dishonour should grow by me, I myself will take up arms—I myself will be your general, judge, and rewarder of every one of your virtues in the field."[1]

The last sovereign to see action in battle was the current Queen's father, George VI. As a 20-year-old sub-lieutenant in the Royal Navy, he fought in the battle of Jutland in 1916. When she was still known as Princess Elizabeth, in 1945 during World War II, Queen Elizabeth II served in the Auxiliary Territorial Service and was the first female member of the Royal Family to be a full-time active member of the armed services. The Queen's husband, The Duke of Edinburgh, served in the Royal Navy from 1939 to 1952 and saw active duty throughout World War II. William's father, Prince Charles, served in the Royal Navy and also trained in the Royal Air Force. Charles's younger brother, Prince Andrew, the Duke of York, served for over 20 years as an officer in the Royal Navy before leaving the military in 2001. He flew as a second pilot in Sea King Helicopters on anti-submarine and transport duties during the Falklands conflict in 1982.

Today, the Queen and the Royal Family have a substantial investment in the Armed Forces as the head of the Armed Forces. For William, as the future king and therefore head of the country's forces, it is necessary to have a military uniform himself. His decision to join the army was an acknowledgement of his royal duty. His grandfather, Prince Philip, strongly urged William to serve in the Royal Navy, noting that it would be a good choice for a future king. However, the months away at sea were not at all appealing, and instead, he chose to enter Sandhurst, the elite military academy, in January 2006. Contributing to his decision to train at Sandhurst was his training with the Welsh Guards on the island of Belize during his gap year. This experience had proved to be meaningful and was one he had never forgotten.

To gain entry to Sandhurst, William had to pass his Regular Commissions Board (RCB), which he did in October 2005. The RCB enables senior army assessors to find those best suited for training and consists of a number of tests and tasks designed to assess mental, physical, and emotional aptitude.

William arrived at Sandhurst accompanied by his father to begin his training course and took his first steps toward accepting his future as head of the armed forces. One instructor at the academy told the assembled media that day that William would get "very little sleep" in the first few weeks of training; he would receive no special treatment, and his drill sergeants would not go easy on him. He explained, "We receive people from all backgrounds, but background goes right out the window once training begins. It's a team effort here. If someone steps out of line they're stamped on, whether they're a prince or not." In the paper the next day, one writer joked that the prince's time at Sandhurst was going to be a "battle of Wills."[2]

As were all of the 269 officer cadets entering the academy that day, William was given a military haircut, which exposed his bald patch, apparently inherited from his father. Known as Officer Cadet Wales, William was assigned to a company and a platoon and was banned from leaving the camp for five weeks. His schedule was grueling; he lived in the field, worked on his physical fitness, and polished his boots until they shined. By the end of the first part of his training, he would be proficient in using a hand grenade, an SA80 5.56mm rifle, and a Browning 9mm pistol. He would also have attended lectures on first aid, military tactics, and war studies. The training would be one of the toughest physical experiences of his life thus far. One challenge came with what was called the "Long Reach," a 24-hour, 40-mile hike with full battle gear across snow-covered hills. Nearly a third of the cadets failed to finish the trek; however, for William, whose own Uncle Edward had been humiliated for washing out of the exercise, failure was not an option.

Harry was already a cadet at Sandhurst and was scheduled to "pass out" or graduate from the academy in April 2006. This meant that William was likely to have to salute his younger brother, something of an embarrassment for most brothers; however, William would do what he must if it meant he could complete his training and still be near his girlfriend, Kate Middleton. In the Navy, William would have had no contact for months with anyone, including Kate. As a trainee officer at Sandhurst, William could invite Kate to military functions, and when he was allowed to leave his barracks, they could spend time together.

After completing his 44-week training course in December 2006, William graduated from the Royal Military Academy Sandhurst. Kate attended his graduation and the Sovereign's Parade with her family. William stood at attention as his grandmother, the Queen, passed by in her formal review and as he was commissioned with the rank of second lieutenant. The Queen spent most of her time seated in the VIP section with Prince Philip, Prince Charles, and Camilla, but all eyes were on Kate, dressed in a scarlet coat and black hat and seated in the general stands. A family friend noted that Kate was attending the ceremony as William's girlfriend and that both of them were tired of all the talk about their becoming engaged, so she had decided to sit apart from the Royal Family. With his officer's commission, William planned to join Harry, already a graduate of Sandhurst, in the company known as the Household Cavalry's Blues and Royals.

Prince William marches with other Sandhurst Military Academy graduates in the Sovereign's Parade, December 15, 2006. (AP Photo/Lewis Whyld, Pool)

As a result of their military training, both William and Harry continually insisted on fighting with their fellow soldiers. As the wars in Iraq and Afghanistan escalated, and there were more terrorist threats to her country, the Queen realized that she could not prevent her grandsons, or at least not both of them, from putting their lives on the line, as was their military duty. The decision to send either or both of them to war would ultimately be made by the military and the government. However, there was a general consensus that the heir to the throne could not be sent to war and put in harm's way. For Harry, it was another matter. After he completed his training, he was put in charge of 4 light tanks and 11 men. Because he was also considered to be a "prize" for any terrorist, the military and the government worried that wherever Harry went in either Iraq or Afghanistan, he would be putting his fellow soldiers in jeopardy. Harry left no doubt that he wanted to be deployed. He used his Uncle Andrew, who had seen combat as a helicopter pilot during the Falklands conflict, as an example. The government at the time had wanted Andrew, then the second in line to the throne, to be transferred to a desk position rather than serve on a helicopter attached to an aircraft carrier. At the time, the Queen remembered how many of her fellow countrymen had put their lives on the line during World War II and intervened, insisting that Andrew be allowed to complete missions along with his fellow naval officers. As always, the Queen was adamant about duty and about sacrifice for country. Harry was confident his grandmother would intervene again. As a lieutenant in the Household Cavalry, Harry served in Afghanistan for more than two months from the end of 2007 to early 2008. And like his older brother, he began training to be a helicopter pilot. For William, military experience has been different. There has been a consensus within the British government that only Harry would be deployed to serve in a combat zone. A veteran British diplomat with close ties to the Royal Family said, "William is the last best hope for the monarchy and the Queen knows it . . . there is simply no way they are going to put him at risk, no matter how much he wants to fight."[3]

Unlike Harry, a career army officer, William also received training in the Royal Air Force and the Royal Navy, all meant to be part of his training in the military service's culture and traditions, as he prepared to head the Armed Forces one day as king. As noted previously, prior to entering Sandhurst for the first part of his military training, he had announced his intention to follow in his father's footsteps and earn his Royal Air Force wings. The first step toward his goal was to learn to fly. In 2008, he went on a four-month attachment with the Royal Air Force (RAF).

On January 17, 2008, William experienced his first solo flight in a light aircraft as he continued his intensive training in the RAF course in Lincolnshire. He joked,

> God knows how somebody trusted me with an aircraft and my own life. It was an amazing feeling, I couldn't believe it. I was doing a few circuits going round and round then Roger my instructor basically turned round and said "right I'm going to jump out now" and I said "what, where are you going?" He said "you're going on your own" and I said "there's no way I'm going to do that" but he said I was ready for it and jumped out. The next thing I knew I was taxiing down the runway and I was sitting there saying "oh my god this is a bit odd, there's no one in here."[4]

William described flying solo as an amazing experience: "Going solo is one of those things—if you had a list of the top 50 things to do before you die, it would be in there." During his attachment Prince William was known as Flying Officer William Wales. And while he was training in the RAF, he remained loyal to the army, but after a few weeks, he came to respect the RAF's professionalism. He said, "My veins run through and through with Army blood. But the RAF have got completely different principles and ethos and are a great bunch of guys and very professional. I relished the opportunity to come and be here."[5]

A fellow officer, Mark Shipley, said of William being one of the flying officers in the course, "It was kind of surreal the first time I met him, but now we play football and have drinks with him. William is working even harder than us because he has got such a short space of time to cover his course." After his initial training, William moved on to the 1 Flying Training School at the Royal Air Force Linton-on-Ouse base in North Yorkshire, where he learned to fly the faster Tucano T1 plane, and then it was on to RAF Shawbury in Shropshire to learn to fly the Squirrel helicopter. William's course was intentionally shortened and

*Britain's Prince William gestures as he walks across
the airfield at RAF Cranwell, Lincolnshire, England,
January 17, 2008. (AP Photo/Kirsty Wigglesworth)*

designed to show him different elements of RAF pilot training; the
course would normally last from three to four years. William, who went
solo after only eight and half hours of flying time, impressed the staff
at 1 Elementary Flying Training School. He also flew in formation with
other aircraft and was described as having natural ability by his instructor. Squadron Leader Bousfield said of his royal student, "To get
William to go solo is fantastic. He's worked very hard and has coped
marvellously [*sic*] to pick it all up and that's been backed up with some
natural talent in the air. He's got good handling skills and learns lessons
really quickly and keeps hold of those lessons, which makes it easier
for the next time we're in the air. His course members have been really
relaxed with him and have got quite attached over the last couple of
weeks."[6]

According to the official Web site for the Prince of Wales,

On April 11, 2008, Prince William received his RAF wings from
his father The Prince of Wales at RAF Cranwell after completing an intensive twelve week flying course; he became the fourth
successive generation of the monarchy to become a Royal Air
Force pilot. On Sunday, April 27th and Monday, April 28th, William undertook a 30-hour trip to RAF Detachments in theatre
at Kandahar Air Base, Afghanistan and Al Udeid, Qatar as the
culmination of his attachment to the RAF. In October 2008, The
Queen appointed new Royal Air Force honorary appointments in
recognition of the strong links between the Royal Air Force and
the Royal Family. Prince William was appointed Honorary Air
Commandant of Royal Air Force Coningsby.[7]

In June 2008, William began a two-month attachment with the
Royal Navy similar to his previous attachment with the Royal Air
Force. Initially, William was stationed on shore at the Britannia Royal
Naval College located in Dartmouth, where he completed a training
course and toured Navy units. There he learned skills that included
navigation, seamanship, and practical boat handling; the course also
included mandatory sea-safety training, in which he learned how to
manage fires aboard ship while wearing a breathing apparatus. His
training also included spending time with the Royal Marines, during
which he learned about amphibious operations and survival training.
Once he completed the first part of his training, William then undertook a second phase that included spending several weeks on the HMS
Iron Duke, a ship that was part of the North Atlantic Patrol and was
stationed in the West Indies providing security for Britain's overseas
territories in the region. As part of the crew on board ship, he was involved in operations to catch drug runners and provide hurricane relief
in the area if needed.

The commander of HMS *Iron Duke*, Commander Mark Newland,
said of William's duties while on board the ship: "His activities will
be primarily based around watch-keeping [and] ship-driving, as well as
contributing to the counter-drugs planning [and] a primary role in our
disaster relief planning operations. But also to educate him in the way

of the Royal Navy. . . . why we are in a theatre of operations like this and what we can do to help." During his time with the Royal Navy, William, as a lieutenant in the British Army, was the equivalent rank of sub-lieutenant and was known as Sub-Lieutenant Wales.[8]

In September 2008, William began his training to become a full-time pilot with the Royal Air Force's Search and Rescue Force (SARF), where he built on the training he had already received to become an operational Sea King pilot. In January 2009, he began his 18-month training course with the RAF to become a fully operational search-and-rescue pilot with one of the six UK-based RAF SARF flights. Prince William began his training in the rank of flying officer, having been commissioned into the air force in January 2008. He transferred his service from the army, in which he was a lieutenant in the Blues and Royals, to the RAF. Prince William said,

> It has been a real privilege to have spent the past year understanding and experiencing all aspects of the British Armed Forces. I now want to build on the experience and training I have received to serve operationally—especially because, for good reasons, I was not able to deploy to Afghanistan this year with D Squadron of the Household Cavalry Regiment. The time I spent with the RAF earlier this year made me realise how much I love flying. Joining Search and Rescue is a perfect opportunity for me to serve in the Forces operationally, while contributing to a vital part of the country's Emergency Services.[9]

In the time available between his training and operational commitments with the Search and Rescue Force, William continued to work with his chosen organizations and charities and also carried out some public royal duties.[10]

The official Web site for the Prince of Wales notes, "In January 2010, William successfully completed his advanced helicopter flying training at the Defence Helicopter Flying School based at RAF Shawbury. The completion of the twelve month course was one important step in his training to become a fully operational pilot with the Royal Air Force's Search and Rescue Force."[11] The next step was to complete the Search and Rescue Conversion Course at the Royal Air Force base in Wales.

In April 2010, it was announced that William would be posted to the RAF Valley base in Anglesey, North Wales, and he would join the Number 22 Squadron, flying a Sea King 3A helicopter. This training included six weeks on the Search and Rescue Training Unit, where he would train in a Griffin helicopter, and then training with the Sea King Operational Conversion Unit, utilizing a mix of simulators and RAF Sea King helicopters. By the summer of 2010, William had completed a series of exercises designed to test the skills acquired in his training, and in late summer 2010, William successfully completed his training and became a fully trained and operational search-and-rescue pilot.

In June 2010, William took part in his first search-and-rescue mission. While flying his helicopter as part of a training sortie, he was diverted to help a climber in Snowdonia. Sadly, William's first taste at rescue ended in tragedy because the climber, suffering from severe head injuries after falling down a mountainside, died. William said, "I did my first mountain rescue the other day. It was amazing after all the training to see it all work in practice. But it was someone with head injuries. Unfortunately, he didn't survive."[12]

The estimated cost to train a search-and-rescue pilot is about £800,000, or approximately $1,221,000. Most helicopter pilots are expected to serve six years, either on two tours of duty in search and rescue or by switching to another air force position before the training costs are recouped. William is aware that if he chooses to leave the Royal Air Force in 2012, after his planned three-year tour of duty as a search-and-rescue helicopter pilot, he will have repaid only about half the cost of training. Advisors to the palace have expected that William would leave the Royal Air Force after one tour of duty and revert to a plan of starting his royal duties on a full-time basis, but this would leave about half the cost of his military training to the taxpayer. The defense department and royal sources have stated that because of this cost, there has been a change of thinking, and William may choose to extend his time in the military. The arguments against William serving in a war zone, based on his line of succession, continue, yet William has always held out hope that he will be able to serve with British forces in Afghanistan. Several scenarios have been discussed, including William switching to flying Chinook helicopters and supporting combat and logistical operations in southern Afghanistan, or he could return to the army, where he has already trained as a Household Cavalry officer, or he might join the Royal Navy, flying helicopters. One source noted, "If you asked William what he plans to do next he would genuinely tell you he has got no firm idea. He could well stay in the military in some capacity. He has said publicly that he would like to serve in Afghanistan. That certainly hasn't been ruled out." A St. James's Palace spokesman stated, "It is too early to know what Prince William's plans are after he has served a tour of duty with the search-and-rescue force. Many options will be open to him at the end of his tour."[13]

Once William completed his search-and-rescue training, he made the decision to remain at Anglesey, a remote, isolated island. This decision, between William and the RAF's chain of command, was based on the fact that remaining at Anglesey would best hone his skills to the challenges of flying over mountainous terrain and hostile seas and supporting both military operations and civilian emergency services in the area. As well, William would one day be taking over his father's role as Prince of Wales, and the posting was designed to bolster the popularity of the monarchy in region. William expects to be promoted to captain and have overall control of the helicopter. He could also find himself flying rescue missions to Northern Ireland from the RAF base in North Wales. A St. James's Palace spokesman said, "The Prince will go wherever he is asked to deploy in the UK including Northern Ireland."[14]

His being posted at the RAF base in North Wales came as somewhat of a surprise. It was expected that William would apply for a transfer to one of the Search and Rescue Force bases in England to be closer to Kate. It was also a surprise in that it was about 80 miles to the nearest fashionable shopping center and a world away from the nightclubs in London. Despite this, Kate Middleton busily mapped out a new life for herself in the Welsh countryside because her future included living in a home where she and William would spend their time together. It could even prove to be their first marital home. In April 2010, one of Kate's friends noted that for the time being, Kate would continue to work at her family's business, Party Pieces, but was likely to spend an increasing amount of time with William in North Wales. William had already moved into a country cottage, complete with his ever-present body guards. Previously, he had lived on the base but had moved in order to have more privacy with Kate as they made plans to begin their life together as a military service couple. As a flight lieutenant and co-pilot, William's salary was around £35,000 a year (approximately $53,000 in U.S. dollars). His schedule included working three 24-hour shifts in a six-day period and sleeping on base while on duty so that he could be airborne within 15 minutes of being called out. In times of emergency, such as widespread flooding, he would be on-call, and it was necessary that he be within an hour of the base. Emergency calls could be dangerous, especially during bad weather, and William could expect to find himself in challenging situations. Search-and-rescue pilots out of the RAF Valley base in Anglesey are expected to carry out the most incredible feats of flying, saving lives during storms at sea or picking up individuals from Snowdonia, a region in north Wales that includes a national park and the highest mountain in Wales, approximately 3,500 feet in elevation. A reporter covering the search-and-rescue teams for the national media, Derek Bellis, said,

> There have been times when they've flown almost blind alongside sheer cliffs, another member of the crew hanging out of the side shouting instructions through the intercom to the pilot. In the bitter sub-zero conditions of last winter rotor blades were often within a few feet of cliffs, aircraft buffeted by gales and down-draughts. Thousands owe their lives to sheer courage and daring, particularly of the pilots and winchmen. Last year the rescue helicopters based at Valley carried out 327 missions, a record. Three-quarters of these were within 35 miles of the base and the vast majority involved mountain rescues.[15]

As a Sea King rescue helicopter pilot, William is expected to live in the Welsh countryside for the duration of his three-year course. As noted previously, his decision to live away from base as much as possible was said to be motivated by wanting more privacy with Kate, even though it was anticipated that she would not live there full-time. As the second in line to the throne, William is classified as the highest security risk, the same as his father and grandmother, the Queen, and he receives round-the-clock armed protection. For him to live off-base, the expense for his protection increases, and taxpayers are asked to pay the annual bill of approximately £1.4 million (or approximately $2.1 million). The living arrangement means North Wales will be involved in providing for his security, along with Scotland Yard, and also means that Wales will lose 15 frontline officers to protecting the future king, unless additional funds can be found to replace them. Anti-monarchy groups were very upset with the expense, stating it was an "appalling waste of taxpayers' money, just as the Royals were being told to cut costs." One member of the anti-monarchy group Republic said, "If William is training as a RAF pilot then he should abide by all the same rules that apply to other trainees. If he feels he is a security risk and doesn't wish to live on base, he should pay for his own security." The North Wales police force was in the midst of budget cuts, and the cost of protecting William was under scrutiny. A former head of Scotland Yard's royal protection squad said of William's decision, "Choosing to live in an isolated cottage in a remote rural area near the port of Holyhead presents all kinds of additional security challenges." A spokesman for Clarence House, Charles and William's official London residence, said, "Prince William has lived off-base for almost two years now and he's lived in this particular cottage since about March. It isn't new. For an officer of his age and rank it is quite normal to live off-base for reasons of privacy."[16]

William is fulfilling his duty as the future sovereign to wear a military uniform. Unlike many of his ancestors, he is more than the inspiration, the motivator, and someone leading from the sidelines; he is actually serving and very much wants to serve and lead on the field of combat, even though he understands his duty and the threats involved in performing in that capacity. While the Queen is currently healthy and expecting to continue to be Her Majesty, and with Charles as the next in line, who is also healthy and waiting to serve his duty as king, William chooses to be in the military. By his service, he is delaying most of the duties as a royal, which many have said is exactly what he wants; however, he does undertake some official royal engagements when he can and serves as a royal in several capacities that are preparing him to be the future king. It is anticipated that the number of engagements is unlikely to increase until he has left the armed forces, which could be years from now, depending on many circumstances. For now, and like some of his ancestors at least, William is doing what he has chosen to do, flying helicopters as part of the armed services and serving his country and performing royal duties as time permits.

WILLIAM'S HUMANITARIAN AND PHILANTHROPIC LIFE

An important part of the work of the Royal Family is to support and encourage public and voluntary service. One of the ways they do this is through involvement with charities and other organizations. According to the official Web site of the British monarchy (www.royalty.gov.uk), members of the Royal Family were lending their names to organizations as long ago as the 18th century. The first patronage was thought to be by George II, who was involved with the Society of Antiquaries, an organization concerned with architecture, art history, conservation, and heraldry that still exists today. Members of the Royal Family are regularly invited to become patrons by a wide range of charities and organizations, and today, approximately 3,000 organizations list a member of the Royal Family as a patron or as president. The Queen alone has approximately 600 patronages, most of which were inherited from her father, King George VI, when she ascended to the throne in 1952. Her husband, the Duke of Edinburgh, has patronages that total over 700.

Although most patronages reflect the individual interests of the individual, often a member of the family will hear about a cause and decide to support it. An example of this is Charles's support of organizations concerned with the environment and the arts. Another example is Camilla's role as president of the National Osteoporosis Society; both her mother and her grandmother died as a result of the disease.

PRINCESS DIANA'S HUMANITARIAN AND CHARITABLE WORKS

Throughout her life, Princess Diana embarked on hundreds of engagements that supported charities and organizations and was president or patron of more than 100 charities. One of her greatest passions was working on behalf of the homeless and disabled and children and adults with HIV/AIDS. She was a patron of Centrepoint, a homeless charity; the English National Ballet; the Leprosy Mission; and the National AIDS Trust. She was also the president of the Hospital for Sick Children, a charity also known as Great Ormond Street, and of the Royal Marsden Hospital. A year before her death, she was an active campaigner for a ban on the manufacture and use of land mines. In January 1997, Diana visited Angola as part of her campaign, and in June of that year, she spoke at the land mines conference at the Royal Geographical Society in London and visited Washington, D.C., to promote the American Red Cross's campaign. She also met with Mother Teresa in New York as part of this appeal.

In 2007, William and Harry organized a concert for their mother called the Concert for Diana, held at Wembley Stadium. Held on July 1, which would have been their mother's 46th birthday, the concert was attended by approximately 62,000 people and was watched on television by millions more around the world. The proceeds of the concert were shared among eight charities, including the Diana, Princess of Wales Memorial Fund, which was founded after Diana's death; Sentebale, the Lesotho children's charity that Prince Harry founded in memory of his mother; and the six organizations of which the princess was a patron at the time of her death: the Royal Marsden and Great Ormond Street Hospitals; Centrepoint, of which Prince William is now a patron; the Leprosy Mission; the National AIDS Trust; and the English National Ballet, who also performed at the concert.[17]

PRINCE CHARLES'S HUMANITARIAN AND CHARITABLE WORKS

Prince Charles is a patron of more than 400 organizations, and many reflect his long-term and innovative perspective on the environment and the arts. The Prince's Charities, specifically, is a group of not-for-profit organizations of which Charles is president; of the 20 charities in the group, Charles personally founded 18. The group of charities is the largest multi-cause charitable enterprise in the United Kingdom, and it raises more than £120 million annually (approximately US$185,000,000). The organizations within the group are active across a broad range of areas, including opportunity, enterprise, education, health, the environment, and the natural environment. Examples of the organizations include the British Asian Trust, the Prince's Drawing School, the Prince's Teaching Institute, the Prince's Foundation for the Built Environment, Business in the Community, Arts & Business, and In Kind Direct. All of the organizations reflect Prince Charles's

long-term and innovative perspective and seek to address areas of previously unmet needs.[18]

WILLIAM'S HUMANITARIAN AND
CHARITABLE WORKS

Even though Prince William has been focusing on his military training for the past few years, as well as his overall training as the future
sovereign, he has continued to follow in his parents' footsteps in the
areas of humanitarianism and charity. As a boy and into his teens, with
his mother, William visited AIDS clinics, shelters, and desperate communities. She was adamant that he learn how other people lived and
how people suffered. Being taken by his mother on a secret visit to see
the homeless living in a shelter as a child led directly to his becoming
the shelter's patron a decade later. In September 2005, William became a patron of the shelter Centrepoint, which Diana had supported
and of which she was a patron until her death. Before he committed
to involvement with the charity, William spent three days volunteering at various Centrepoint hostels throughout London. The CEO of
Centrepoint said of William, "He has real empathy with people in general, but especially those his own age. Like his mother, he obviously
cares and he's a good listener. People feel of more value when they see
that our future King wants to spend time with them. Still, it can be a
bit startling when you come into the kitchen all sleepy-eyed and find
Prince William making your coffee."[19]

In December 2009, after receiving a challenge from Centrepoint's
CEO, William spent a night sleeping in subzero temperatures on the
streets of London, bedding down in an old sleeping bag in a doorway
with no more than cardboard boxes to ease his discomfort. Dressed in
jeans, athletic shoes, a hooded top, and a woolly hat, William slept
near the Blackfriars Bridge with a police body guard stationed discreetly
nearby. Although it was a challenge that was not expected to be taken,
the charity has long been one close to the prince's heart and that of his
late mother too.[20] For William, it was an opportunity to raise the profile
of the charity and to discover what the realities are for the homeless.
It was also a lesson in the dangers that the homeless face. This danger
became a reality when he, the charity's chief executive, and his private

secretary narrowly avoided being run over by a road sweeper. William noted later, "I cannot, after one night, even begin to imagine what it must be like to sleep rough night after night." He added that the shelter is doing the essential work to tackle the fundamental causes of homelessness: poverty, mental illness, drug and alcohol dependency, and family breakdown. He hoped the experience would help him to "do my bit to help the most vulnerable." The CEO of the organization, Seyi Obakin, wrote on the organization's Web site, "For me, it was a scary experience. Out of my comfortable bed. Out there in the elements. And it was the same for Prince William."

William shows his support for many organizations beside Centrepoint, organizations that reflect the issues he cares about, both in the United Kingdom and abroad. He is patron or president of the following organizations: the Child Bereavement Charity, the English Schools' Swimming Association, the Football Association, the Henry Van Straubenzee Memorial Fund, the HMS Alliance Conservation Appeal, Mountain Rescue (England and Wales), A Positive View 2010, Royal Air Force Battle of Britain Memorial Flight, the Royal Marsden Hospital, Skill Force, the Tusk Trust, and the Welsh Rugby Union.[21] The official Web site for the British monarchy states, "In December 2005, William became Patron of the Tusk Trust, a conservation charity based in the UK which aims to secure a peaceful co-existence for Africa's wildlife and its people. Prince William was impressed by the work of the charity after seeing it first-hand during a visit to Africa."[22]

According to the official Web site for the Prince of Wales, and as noted previously, in May 2006, William became president of the Football Association, the governing body of English football. He took over the organization from his uncle, the Duke of York. The Web site also notes,

In May 2007, William became President of the Royal Marsden Hospital, a position previously held by his mother, Diana, the Princess of Wales. Throughout his life, he visited the hospital many times, and in December 2005, he undertook two days of work experience there, helping out in a variety of departments that included medical research, catering, and fund-raising, as well as visiting a number of wards, including the Children's Unit. Also in May 2007,

William became the Patron of Mountain Rescue England and Wales and The English Schools' Swimming Association. These patronages reflect William's interest in youth sport and, in his own words, his desire to highlight and celebrate the vital, selfless and courageous work of our mountain rescue organisations.[23]

THE FOUNDATION OF PRINCE WILLIAM AND PRINCE HARRY

Without a doubt, both Prince William and Prince Harry are recognized throughout the world, and they both understand the good work they can do to help others. They also believe it is very important for them to carry on their parents' philanthropic efforts and help the less fortunate. This is what they were taught growing up and what they continue to do as members of the Royal Family. To that end, they established the Foundation of Prince William and Prince Harry in September 2009, an organization that enables both of them to further their charitable ambitions.

Because both William and Harry are patrons or presidents of many charities and organizations throughout the United Kingdom and abroad, in order to foster greater collaborations among their many affiliations, they created the Princes' Charities Forum in 2006. After their successes in raising funds and awareness with the Concert for Diana in 2007 and with the City Salute, which raised money for Headley Court military hospital and the Soldiers, Sailors, Airmen and Families Association, their foundation was the culmination of their charitable lives. The intent was to have a vehicle for their future charitable activities and to raise a self-sustaining endowment fund to make charitable grants. Prince William said,

> We are incredibly excited about our new Foundation. We believe that it will provide a unique opportunity for us, as brothers, to use our privileged position to make a real difference in the future to many areas of charitable work. At present, and over the years ahead, we are committing ourselves to three particular areas: doing all that we possibly can to help the most disadvantaged young people in our society; raising awareness of and support for

our Servicemen and women who put their lives on the line for this Country; and backing true innovation and initiative in the critical work being done to develop sustainable models of life and society in the light of climate change and dwindling natural resources. We feel passionately that, working closely together with those who contribute to our Foundation, we can help to make a long-lasting and tangible difference.[24]

According to the official Web site for the Foundation of Prince William and Prince Harry, the areas of focus are

young People, particularly those of their own age and younger who are disadvantaged or in need of guidance and support at a crucial time in their lives; the environment, particularly to build on the growing awareness of the need to find better, more sustainable, models to balance development and the conservation of resources; and the armed forces, for the welfare of those who serve their country in the Armed Forces, particularly looking after those who return broken in body or mind—or not at all— and their families.[25]

Regarding the future of the foundation, in January 2010, William said, "We are incredibly lucky, Harry and I. We know that. But both our father and our mother instilled in us, from the word go, that with these great privileges goes an absolute responsibility to give back." Prince Harry said, "We are both massively excited at the prospect of being able to help in whatever way we can, where we can. As Prince William said, if we can use our position to do this, we are ready to."[26]

NOTES

1. The Official Web Site of the British Monarchy, "History and Background," http://www.royal.gov.uk/MonarchUK/ArmedForces/History.aspx (accessed July 16, 2010).

2. Robert Jobson, *William's Princess* (London: John Blake, 2006), 190.

3. Christopher Andersen, *After Diana* (New York: Hyperion, 2007), 296.

4. Prince of Wales Web site. "Prince William Flies Solo during his RAF Attachment," http://www.princeofwales.gov.uk/newsandgallery/news/prince_william_flies_solo_during_his_raf_attachment_424384859.html (accessed January 20, 2011).

5. Prince of Wales Web Site, "The Wedding Of HRH Prince William Of Wales And Miss Catherine Middleton—An Update," http://www.princeofwales.gov.uk/newsandgallery (accessed July 20, 2010).

6. Ibid.

7. Official Web Site of the British Monarchy, "Military Career," http://www.royal.gov.uk/ThecurrentRoyalFamily/PrinceWilliam/Militarycareer.aspx (accessed July 19, 2010).

8. Prince of Wales Web Site, "Prince William to Become Patron of the Imperial War Museum Foundation's First World War Centenary Appeal," http://www.princeofwales.gov.uk/mediacentre/pressreleases (accessed July 20, 2010).

9. Prince of Wales Web site. "Prince William to Join RAF Search and Rescue," http://www.princeofwales.gov.uk/mediacentre/pressreleases/prince_william_to_join_raf_search_and_rescue_1291894627.html (accessed January 20, 2011).

10. Official Web Site of the British Monarchy, "Military Career," http://www.royal.gov.uk/ThecurrentRoyalFamily/PrinceWilliam/Militarycareer.aspx (accessed July 19, 2010).

11. Prince of Wales Web site, "Military Career," http://www.princeofwales.gov.uk/personalprofiles/princewilliamprinceharry/princeiwlliam/atwork/militarycareer/index.html (accessed December 9, 2010).

12. Richard Palmer, "Prince William Sent on First Real-Life Emergency Mission as Climber Dies," *Daily Express*, June 7, 2010. http://www.express.co.uk (accessed July 21, 2010).

13. Richard Palmer, "Prince William May Put Off Royal Duties to Keep Flying," *Daily Express*, March 22, 2010. http://www.express.co.uk (accessed July 21, 2010).

14. Richard Palmer, "William's RAF Posting Announced," *Daily Express*, April 15, 2010. http://www.express.co.uk (accessed July 21, 2010).

15. Richard Palmer, "Royal Blog: Prince William and Kate Middleton's New Life in the Welsh Countryside," *Daily Express*, April 16, 2010. http://www.express.co.uk (accessed July 21, 2010).

16. Lianne Kolirin, "Prince William under Fire over £1.4m Bill to Guard His Cottage," *Daily Express*, July 19, 2010. http://www.express.co.uk (accessed July 19, 2010).

17. Official Web Site of the British Monarchy, http://www.royal.gov.uk (accessed July 26, 2010).

18. Ibid.

19. Jumana Farouky, "Like Mother, Like Sons," *Time International* (Europe Edition) 170, no. 8 (2007): 22.

20. Low Valentine, "From Prince to Pauper: How William Spent the Night on the Freezing Streets of London," *Times*, December 23, 2009, 3 (accessed February 4, 2010).

21. Official Web Site of the British Monarchy, http://www.royal.gov.uk (accessed July 26, 2010).

22. Official Web Site of the British Monarchy, "Charities and Patronages," http://www.royal.gov.uk/ThecurrentRoyalFamily/PrinceWilliam/charitiesandpatronages.aspx (accessed December 10, 2010).

23. Prince of Wales Web Site, "Charities and Patronages," http://www.princeofwales.gov.uk/personalprofiles/princewilliamprinceharry/princewilliam/atwork/charitiesandpatronages/index.html (accessed December 10, 2010).

24. Prince of Wales Web Site, http://www.princeofwales.gov.uk (accessed July 21, 2010).

25. Prince of Wales Web Site, "The Foundation of Prince William and Prince Harry," http://www.princeofwales.gov.uk/newsandgallery/focus/the_foundation_of_prince_william_and_prince_harry_570302665.html (accessed December 10, 2010).

26. Ibid.

Chapter 9

THE FUTURE KING

She's been brilliant, she's a real role model.

—*Prince William on his grandmother, the Queen*

Just as the world has changed, the monarchy has changed since Queen Elizabeth II ascended to the throne in 1952. One impetus for the many changes was the effect Princess Diana, often referred to the People's Princess, had on the Royals and the monarchy itself. For many, she made the monarchy more relevant and in touch with the commoners of the Commonwealth. The monarchy has also been pushed into economizing and cutting expenses. As recently as July 2010, the Queen had to make plans for how the palace could generate income and economize to decrease expenses, including freezing salaries of Buckingham Palace employees, forgoing repairs to the palace and Windsor Castle, and reviewing whether open positions should be filled. The monarchy has instituted additional commercialization of the monarchy through more gift shops selling trinkets and gifts and by opening the royal residences to the paying public to increase revenues.

For William, these changes, along with an increase in exposure of the Royal Family to the public, could mean increased exposure of his personal life, something the often camera-shy and fiercely private prince may not like. It is certain that William is and will continue to be an icon, a man who will always represent the monarchy, and he will continue what his mother began by being relevant to a more diverse society and to a rapidly changing nation and world. Critics believe the monarchy is not at all relevant today and state that members of the Royal Family are not held in the same esteem as they once were. They also contend that the costs of the monarchy, including the expenses to maintain the properties and the tax exemptions granted to the Queen and some members of the family, are unnecessary and unsupportable. Critics state the monarchy should be abolished and replaced by a republic, something that has been discussed and supported since the 1870s. Supporters of the monarchy are calling for a more active role for their queen or king, even to the extent of having the monarch play a more active role in making government policy and exercising political will. If Queen Elizabeth II dies and Charles becomes King, and if Charles leaves the throne for any reason and William is crowned King, both Charles and his eldest son will inherit a much different monarchy from the one Elizabeth inherited from her father, King George VI. Changes to the relevancy of the monarchy and the Royal Family itself have been in motion for many years, and what the Royals will do to encourage continuous change and answer their critics who wish to abolish the monarchy remains to be seen. In the end, however, the British monarchy's durability remains intact and to some still defies explanation.

For centuries, the queen or king sitting on the royal throne has been thought of as magical and enduring. If Charles becomes king, he is expected to be a more modern monarch than his mother, as well as considerably more informal and more accessible to the people. However, Charles is very much like his mother and his ancestors in that he likes to dress for dinner, he is more than just nostalgic for the kind of life the Royals used to have, and he still enjoys the pampered luxuries afforded him. He is steeped in the traditions of the monarchy.

Of Charles's son, Hugo Vickers, a royal historian, has said, "William is really the great hope of the future. He's got the heritage of his mother and his father. He could unite the two factions."[1] William was raised and trained to be a royal from the first moment of his birth. He was raised by a mother who felt he should have as normal a life as was possible. Diana insisted on giving both her sons a sense of their value as people rather than as princes. William's father had great influence on him too, including wanting his sons to show concern for people and their circumstances and refusing to allow his sons to be tied to all the royal traditions, providing them freedoms that even he never had. Unfortunately, there is a limit to how much privacy and freedom William can ever have, despite both his parents' wishes. For the Royals in general and certainly for the man in line to the throne, there is very little private life. And though he remains a very private person who understands his destiny and duty, he also prefers there be no fuss and no special attention given him. And though this will likely change in the future, especially when and if Charles becomes king and William is second in line to the throne, he has always shunned being called His Royal Highness, or even Prince William; rather, he prefers Wills or just William. He does not take to people bowing or curtsying in front of him, and he would very much like to be himself and do what he pleases as much as possible.

William has always avoided and been uncomfortable with attention and has made decisions that have purposely kept him out of the limelight and away from as many royal duties as possible. However, there is no escape for William; he was born to be king. Throughout history, few have had their destinies so completely decided for them, and few have had so little self-determination. As a boy, when he was told he would someday be king, this news may have been exciting; the prospect of doing whatever he pleased may have sounded like fun. But as he grew into his teenage years and into adulthood, the enormity of the responsibilities must have been daunting, especially when he was so close to his parents and watched their lives be so gravely impacted by being a member of the Royal Family. He watched his parents' divorce, and he publicly mourned his mother's untimely death. Yet he has persevered, as has been expected of him.

The Queen, who has seen her own tragedies and has lived through difficult times personally and as Queen, has kept her dignity and been stout in her duty. She expects the same for her grandson, the future king. For William, what has been a challenge is forging a meaningful adult identity in a world where the monarchy is becoming less relevant. And although the Queen, as of 2010 at least, enjoys good health and has seemingly no intention of abdicating her throne and bypassing her own son, it has been speculated that she is pinning her hopes on her grandson. A royal insider stated, "She has been known to say that it's William who will take the monarchy into the 21st century. William and Harry together, actually, because he needs the support of his brother."[2] The real focus and hope for the future appear to be on William. For some time, the Queen has been spending more time with him, and he is taking on a few more roles, even though he has been reluctant to do so. He went to Sandhurst and continued his military training and now wears the required military uniform. He is prepared to someday be the head of the armed forces. He is president of the Football Association, a role he took over from his uncle, Prince Andrew. His association with this national sport of the United Kingdom is one that both George V and George VI also held and were said to very much enjoy. Over all, William is preparing to be a modern monarch. For all his privileged life, he remains as his mother and father wanted: a man of the people.

Charles once said, "To me the object of life is not to pursue personal happiness. It sounds ridiculously self-righteous and trite, but I would rather pursue other people's happiness." And it appears William agrees and intends to do the same. The way he does it will be all his own, however. As Charles acknowledges, "He will no doubt have his own outlook and his own way of doing things, which wouldn't be exactly the same as mine by any means."[3] William is independent and has held his ground on many of his decisions. This does not allow him to discard completely what has gone before him. Continuity is fundamental to the monarchy's role in the Commonwealth. William, like his father and his grandmother, knows and appreciates this.

To mark his 21st birthday in 2003, William used an interview to assert his desire to serve his country and rebut a claim that he never wanted to be king:

> All these questions about "Do you want to be king?" It's not a question of wanting to be, it's something I was born into and it's my duty . . . It's an important role and it's one that I don't take lightly. It's all about helping people and dedication and loyalty which I hope I have—I know I have . . . I'll take each step as it comes and deal with it as best I can. The monarchy is something

that needs to be there—I just feel it's very, very important—it's a form of stability and I hope to be able to continue that.[4]

He is his own man, however. He is determined to make his own decisions. He signaled his strong-mindedness in an interview with London's *Mail on Sunday's Live* magazine in early 2010. When asked if he had to accept that there would always be people dictating what he could and could not do, he replied, "No. That's the thing. I like to disagree with them deliberately, because many of the things they come up with are very old-fashioned and don't work nowadays or are just wrong . . . Sometimes I listen to people but I like to take in lots of opinions and then make my own judgment."[5]

It is the crown that defines him, and the responsibilities he faces now and in the future are tremendous. He will use his grandmother's strength and sense of duty, his father's passions and love of traditions, and his mother's compassion and position as one of the people; and he will know that in the end, he has no choice but to succeed on his own.

NOTES

1. "Prince Charming," *Newsweek*, June 25, 2000, 44.

2. "Prince Charming: Sporty, Swoon-Worthy and Strikingly Sensible as They Approach Adulthood, William and Harry Do Both Their Parents Proud," *People Weekly*, April 24, 2000, 98+.

3. Ingrid Seward, *William and Harry* (New York: Arcade, 2003), 294, 295.

4. Robert Jobson, *William's Princess* (London: John Blake, 2006), 240.

5. Katie Nicholl, "Palace Frustrated and Queen Left in the Dark as Prince William Insists on Taking Charge of Wedding Plans," *Mail Online*, November 21, 2010.

BIBLIOGRAPHY

Andersen, Christopher. *After Diana*. New York: Hyperion, 2007.

Andersen, Christopher. *Diana's Boys*. New York: William Morrow, 2001.

Bernstein, Fred. "William the Terrible: Di's Darling Is a Precocious Tot Who Can Be a Royal Pain." *People Weekly*, July 7, 1986, 106+.

Brown, Tina. *The Diana Chronicles*. New York: Doubleday, 2007.

Cannon, John, and Ralph Griffiths. *The Oxford Illustrated History of the British Monarchy*. Oxford, England: Oxford University Press, 1988.

Centre Point. http://www. centrepoint.org.uk. Accessed June 24, 2010.

Eton College. http://www.eatoncollege.com.

The FA. http://www.thefa.com. Accessed June 28, 2010.

Farouky, Jumana. "Like Mother, Like Sons." *Time International* (Europe Edition) 170, no. 8 (2007).

Graham, Tim, and Peter Archer. *William: HRH Prince William of Wales*. New York: Atria Books, 2003.

Green, Michelle. "A Royal First." *People Weekly*, June 27, 1983, 89+.

Hoey, Brian. *Prince William*. Phoenix Mill, England: Sutton, 2003.

Jobson, Robert. *William's Princess*. London: John Blake, 2006.

Jost, Kenneth. "The British Monarchy." *CQ Researcher Online* 6, no. 9 (March 8, 1996): 193–216. http://library.cqpress.com/cqresearcher/cqresrre1996030800.

Katz, Gregory. "Prince William, Kate Middleton Royal Wedding?" *Huffington Post*, November 10, 2010. http://www.huffingtonpost.com.

Kaufman, Joanne. "Happy Birthday, Prince Charming." *People Weekly*, June 26, 1989, 30+.

Kolirin, Lianne. "Prince William under Fire over £1.4m Bill to Guard His Cottage." *Daily Express*, July 19, 2010. http://www.express.co.uk.

Lee, Robert Mason. "William Takes a Bride?" *Maclean's*, August 15, 2005, 40–41.

Min, Janice. "Prince Dreamboat." *People Weekly*, July 1, 1996, 72+.

Nicholl, Katie. "Palace Frustrated and Queen Left in the Dark as Prince William Insists on Taking Charge of Wedding Plans." *Mail Online*, November 21, 2010. http://www.dailymail.co.uk.

Official Web Site of the British Monarchy. http://www.royal.gov.uk. Accessed July 26, 2010.

Palmer, Richard. "Prince William May Put Off Royal Duties to Keep Flying." *Daily Express*, March 22, 2010. http://www.express.co.uk.

Palmer, Richard. "Prince William Sent on First Real-Life Emergency Mission as Climber Dies." *Daily Express*, June 7, 2010. http://www.express.co.uk.

Palmer, Richard. "Royal Blog: Prince William and Kate Middleton's New Life in the Welsh Countryside." *Daily Express*, April 16, 2010. http://www.express.co.uk.

Palmer, Richard. "William's RAF Posting Announced." *Daily Express*, April 15, 2010. http://www.express.co.uk.

Perry, Simon, et al. "Separate Ways," *People*, April 30, 2007, 96–103.

"Prince Charming." *Newsweek*, June 25, 2000, 44.

"Prince Charming: Sporty, Swoon-Worthy and Strikingly Sensible as They Approach Adulthood, William and Harry Do Both Their Parents Proud." *People Weekly*, April 24, 2000, 98+.

Prince of Wales. http://www.princeofwales.gov.uk. Accessed June 26, 2010.

"Prince William Should Be Next King." *The Daily Beast*, November 21, 2010. http://www.thedailybeast.com.

"The Rising Son: Diana and Charles's Oldest Boy Emerges from Childhood." *People Weekly*, July 3, 2000, 56+.

Seward, Ingrid. *William and Harry*. New York: Arcade, 2003.

Spencer, Earl. "The Eulogy." *Newsweek*, September 15, 1997.

Tauber, Michelle. "Frosh Prince: Part Swinger, Part 'Swot'." *People Weekly*, November 5, 2001, 88.

Tresniowki, Alex, et al. "Boys to Men." *People*, June 4, 2007, 88–94.

The Tusk Trust. http://www.tusk.org. Accessed June 24, 2010.

Valentine, Low. "From Prince to Pauper: How William Spent the Night on the Freezing Streets of London." *Times*, December 23, 2009, 3.

Wilkinson, Philip. *The British Monarchy for Dummies*. Chichester, West Sussex, England: Wiley, 2006.

INDEX

About the Author

JOANN F. PRICE is a professional writer, writing coach, and instructor of English with more than 20 years in academic and business settings. For the past eight years, she has taught writing and research skills at Metropolitan State College of Denver. She is the author of *Martha Stewart: A Biography*; *Barack Obama: A Biography*; and *Barack Obama, Voice of an American Leader*. Her essay on caregiving, titled "Taking Care," appeared in two volumes of the Healing Project's "Voices of" series (LaChance Publishing). She spends her time with her family, writing, reading, planning trips, and traveling as much as possible.